RECESSION-RESISTANT READINESS VOLUME 01

GROW PROFIT OR DIE

Thanks to my Red Wagon Advisors Team

Copyright © 2024 by Wade Wyant All rights reserved.

No part of this book may be reproduced in any form or by any electronic or mechanical means, including information storage and retrieval systems, without written permission from the author, except for the use of brief quotations in a book review.

Title: Grow profit or die: recession-resistant readiness volume 1 / Wade W. Wyant; edited by Melissa Main; illustrated by Leah Buchanan.

Description: Includes bibliographical references. | Grand Rapids, MI: Jaatoo, 2024.
Identifiers: ISBN: 979-8857040133 (print)

Subjects: LCSH Entrepreneurship. | Success in business. | Leadership. | Management. | Recession. | Small business. | BISAC BUSINESS & ECONOMICS / Mentoring & Coaching | BUSINESS & ECONOMICS / Entrepreneurship | BUSINESS & ECONOMICS / Leadership

Grow Profit or Die: Recession-Resistant Readiness Advanced Readers Copy Uncorrected v10

Contents

Preface 01

Introduction 03

Chapter 1: Planning 15

Chapter 2: Preparation 33

Chapter 3: Agenda 63

Chapter 4: A "How To" on the Sections of the Agenda 77

Chapter 5: Conclusion 119

About the Author 123

Notes 125

Glossary 137

Resources 143

Recession-Resistant Start Up Guide 149

Recession-Resistant Infograph 163

Wake-Up Call Articles 169

Citations 187

Preface

Two years ago, when I penned my book *Wake-Up Call,* I introduced a groundbreaking concept: it's not merely *grow or die*, but rather *grow profit or die*. Following the publication, the significance of this notion became increasingly evident. Concurrently, the term *recession* began to surface frequently in the media, and by the end of 2022, a majority of business leaders were convinced that a recession was imminent. In tandem with these developments, I had been contemplating a book or workshop on the subject of *growing profit*. With an outline forming in my mind and the prospect of an impending recession, I realized I had an opportunity to address both issues simultaneously. Thus, I embarked on the journey of writing a book on growing profit while aiding business leaders in bracing for the approaching recession.

And so, this book was born.

Profit is consistently crucial. However, businesses occasionally choose to sacrifice it for various reasons, such as growth, environmental initiatives, tax considerations, or in many instances, a lack of discipline. But when a recession looms, the necessity to regain profitability and adopt a lean approach becomes paramount. Many of the principles required to grow profit also directly contribute to preparing for a recession.

In collaboration with my team, we identified several fundamental actions needed to brace for a recession. Intriguingly, many of these measures demanded not only discovery, but also a commitment from a company's leadership team to pause, strategize, and implement the required changes now, as well as plan for adjustments during the recession. This epiphany inspired the creation of this book.

Our primary objective was to craft a book that empowers readers to prepare and conduct a successful planning session or workshop for a future recession. We understand that facilitating this type of planning can be challenging.

Therefore, as a professional services company, our secondary aim is to extend our support to you. If you are interested in collaborating with a professional to assist you in conducting a workshop or planning session, please refer to our contact information at the end of this book. We eagerly anticipate learning how this workbook bolsters your profit growth and equips you for any future recession. We encourage you to share your feedback online and stay tuned for an updated version with additional content in our *Grow Profit or Die* workbooks.

Warmly,

— WADE.

-W.

Introduction

As you delve into this book, you'll find that it equips your business with the tools to brace for a recession, without prescribing specific actions during a recession. We have experience in both growing companies' profits during prosperous times and navigating past recessions, so we can provide you with a comprehensive resource.

As mentioned in the preface, you can utilize this guide in any manner you see fit. We recommend initially using it as a discovery tool. Then use it as a blueprint for conducting recession-preparation planning sessions or a full-day workshop with your team. This book will prepare you to be equipped for a future recession.

We believe the number #1 thing nearly all businesses need headed into any economic challenge is better profitability.

What if we never have a recession?

As we finish writing this book, it is important to not miss an important point. What if we never have another recession or don't have one in the 2020s? It is possible. We have gone this long without a recession, and the major world governments seem satisfied with manipulating their economies to avoid a recession. However, at Red Wagon, we believe strongly that a recession will hit between 2024 and 2025. Late 2024 is probably the most likely target based on the U.S. election cycle.

In the off chance that we don't have another recession, we believe this workbook is still critical for any team to explore. Not only does it prepare you for a recession, but it also prepares you for the ultimate goal: *Grow Profit*. All the activities you will go through and actions you will take as a result of this workbook will help you grow more profitably and with less risk.

Whatever your beliefs are on the future of the U.S. economy and the need to prepare for a recession, going through the activities in this workbook will be of great value. Even just reviewing this book and absorbing some of the concepts will help mature your business and grow profit. So, we encourage you to keep reading and look forward to learning how it helps your company.

Regarding the full day workshop:

At Red Wagon, we firmly believe that a one or two-day workshop is the most effective approach to preparing for a potential recession. However, if this format doesn't align with your company's meeting style or collaboration preferences, you can easily adapt it to suit your needs. You could break the workshop into multiple sessions, assign a dedicated team to handle the preparations, or incorporate it as a recurring segment in your weekly meetings over a few months. The key is to prioritize planning and **ensure you are prepared**!

For the entrepreneur or CEO who likes to go it alone, this workbook can also serve as a guide to what you need to think about or prepare for as we approach a future recession.

At Red Wagon, we provide you with the resources to grow and sustain your profit. We endeavored to write this book to give you the tools and framework to accomplish this mission.

"Grow Profit or Die"

The remainder of the introduction is intended to offer techniques to kickstart the process and motivate your team. If you do not feel like you need this, please feel free to go directly to Chapter 1.

The Call to Action

Companies and their leadership teams who invest the time and resources in preparing for a recession are setting themselves up for success in the event of an economic downturn. They are also taking steps to improve their overall business operations and competitiveness. By using this book, companies will prepare for a recession by reviewing and refining current business practices, which can ultimately lead to greater efficiency, effectiveness, and a more resilient company.

By being proactive and doing the necessary prework, companies and their teams will gain a deeper understanding of the effects of a recession, allowing them to make informed and strategic decisions. This workbook highlights potential pivots or changes that could add revenue or profit to the business. These pivots may be difficult or impossible to implement during a recession. Workshops and planning sessions further increase the effectiveness of this book. Also, the hands-on experience will empower teams to think beyond the recession and to be better prepared for any future economic challenges.

> *"By being proactive and doing the necessary prework, companies and their teams will gain a deeper understanding of the effects of a recession, allowing them to make informed and strategic decisions."*

Making the decision today to invest in this work and doing the necessary prework is not only worth it in the short-term — as it will help companies prepare for and potentially thrive during a recession — but it also has long-term benefits for the overall health of the business.

Why Take the Time?

Much like other aspects of life, sustaining a company over an extended period requires discipline. During prosperous times, managing a business may seem effortless, leading to complacency. We see this play out in low profit, over staffing, and poor inventory control. However, inevitably, all economies and businesses face periods of subpar performance. Regrettably, many business leaders are unprepared for these downturns, causing their companies to suffer more than necessary.

Drawing on the insights we have gleaned from writing the book *Wake-Up Call*, our objective is to provide you with the tools needed to prepare for an eventual economic downturn. In times of decline, panic often ensues, resulting in hasty and ill-informed decision-making. The key to success during such periods is proactive preparation, allowing for well-considered decisions that yield more favorable outcomes.

Teams may neglect to engage in this process for several reasons. First, time constraints can be an issue, which can be resolved through prioritization. Second, some may prefer to avoid confronting these challenges, opting instead to remain in a state of blissful ignorance. This attitude requires discipline to overcome, much like resisting unhealthy eating habits. Finally, teams may need guidance to undertake this crucial process. Therefore, we have developed this resource to fill that void, offering guidance and posing essential questions for consideration.

The underlying *why* behind creating this tool is to equip you for the challenges ahead. Your motivation for utilizing it should be simple: you want to be prepared.

Some may prefer to avoid confronting these challenges, opting instead to dwell in a state of blissful ignorance.

> ***Pro Tip*** *– Many of these tools from GPOD will enable you to run better weekly and quarterly meetings. Like the structure you get from Scaling Up[1] and Traction[2], GPOD brings better accountability to the team.*

EXERCISE 1
www.growprofitordie.com

GROW PROFIT OR DIE

Let's get started. After reading this section, it is likely that your subconscious has thought of several areas where you could begin working. These will be great to bring up in the working session with your team or even start correcting now. Don't miss this opportunity to get those thoughts or ideas on paper.

Top People or Departments That Are Understaffed

1 _____

2 _____

3 _____

Top Deals or Services with Low Gross Profit You Need To Fix

1 _____

2 _____

3 _____

Every Business Carries Some Type of Inventory. Where Are You Overcomitted?

1 _____

2 _____

3 _____

Ways to Sell Your Team on the Need to Prepare for Any Up-Coming Recession

In many cases your team may not be convinced they need to plan for a recession or take the time to do this work. We want to arm you with some additional reasons for doing pre-planning as you are justifying this extra work to your team.

There are several compelling reasons why a company and its leadership team would want to read this workbook and conduct a recession-resistant workshop with their team. Here are a few of the key reasons:

Better Decision Making: By proactively preparing for a recession, companies and their leadership teams can make informed and strategic decisions, rather than panicked and reactive ones. This can lead to better outcomes and a more resilient business.

Improved Business Operations: The work done to prepare for a recession can have a positive impact on overall business operations, regardless of whether a recession actually occurs. This is because the preparation process often involves reviewing and refining business practices, which can lead to improved efficiency and effectiveness.

Peace of Mind: Preparing for a recession can give employees and investors peace of mind, knowing that the company is proactively addressing potential challenges and is taking steps to minimize risks. This can improve employee morale and investor confidence.

> *With the challenges of mental health in today's world, do you want to add additional anxiety to your workplace during an economic downturn or recession by not being ready?*

Competitive Advantage: By being better prepared for a recession, companies may be able to take advantage of opportunities that others cannot, positioning them for success during and after the recession.

Increased Understanding: Running this process will expand your understanding of a recession and give you more confidence. This deeper understanding can help your team better navigate the economic challenges that may arise.

Strategic Pivots: The planning and workshop will reveal pivots or changes in the business that could add revenue or profit. These types of shifts are often difficult or impossible to make during a recession, making it all the more important to address them before the economic conditions worsen.

Hands-On Learning: Beyond the understanding you will gain, the hands-on experience of conducting the workshop will empower your team to think beyond the recession and help them develop the skills and knowledge necessary to navigate economic challenges.

EXERCISE 2

www.growprofitordie.com

GROW PROFIT OR DIE

It's likely you will have to convince members of the team that recession-resistant preparation is worth doing. Most teams want to avoid this work. If you are committed to preparing for a recession, make a list of why you are doing it.

Decide now, will this be a one-day event? Will it occur over a few meetings? Will a group of people or just one person attend?

List Your Top 5 Reasons for Doing Recession-Resistant Preparation:

1 _____

2 _____

3 _____

4 _____

5 _____

What's the best way for your team to tackle it?

A. Workshop

B. Weekly Meetings

C. Project

D. Have One Person Doing It

In summary, conducting a recession-resistant readiness process with your team and using this workbook as a guide can help your company better prepare for potential economic challenges and position your business for long-term success.

> *Pivots are nearly impossible to pull off during a recession. We can tell you from experience that your natural reaction will be to pivot to something new. However, in many cases, it is a waste of time if you didn't get started prior to the downturn. If you have a potential pivot or think you'll need one, start the process now to have the additional business in place when the recession hits.*

A note from the author: *In one of my past businesses, I worked in cybersecurity. The early evolution of our business was managing computers on networks and applying security patches. We had this amazing software we used called Altiris. It was a game changer and companies wanted it. Our primary service was installing and configuring the software to work on their network with their computers. At first glance, you would think most company networks would be configured and run in a similar way. I can tell you that is NOT the case. Despite being IT professionals who were involved in the installation and configuration of the software and should have known better, we still assumed this falsehood.*

We would always start our engagements with the statement: "This software is incredible and powerful. It can automate much of the work you do manually today. The challenge is that if you have any issues or have taken any shortcuts in your IT department, it will find them." We would always say that and always be reassured by the client that there was nothing they could think of that would be an issue. We would then spend the next few days finding every bug and misconfiguration they had been hiding, ignoring, or putting off for the past 10 years. Every time we would find something new, they would look at us wide eyed and say something like, "Oh, yeah, we forgot about that problem." This happened so much we would just build time in for it. Thinking back, we should have charged more for this feature.

Why do I tell you this story? The tools, Pro Tips, best practices and exercises we share in this book will create a very similar scenario to the story above. As you work through this material, you will find many areas or challenges in your business that you have very likely put off for months or years. This is an extra benefit to going through this larger exercise, but it is also a cost. So be prepared and be warned as you continue to read.

Chapter 1 - Planning

Part 1 - Planning Your Workshop

When it comes to preparing your business for a potential recession, it's important to approach the process with a clear and well-thought-out plan. Winging it or simply hoping for the best is not a strategy for success. To achieve the desired outcomes, you must take the time to plan your workshop and to ensure that you have the right resources and approach in place.

In this first chapter of the book, we will guide you through the planning process and provide you with the tools and resources you need to prepare for successful meetings, where you will discover ways to increase profitability. Whether you're a seasoned business professional or just starting out, you'll find valuable information and guidance in this chapter that will help you to plan and execute a workshop that meets your needs and the needs of your business.

Part 2 - The Importance of an Agenda

One of the key components of planning the collaborative work with your team is developing an agenda that works for your business. This agenda should outline the topics that you plan to cover either in a full-day workshop or across several meetings. The agenda should highlight activities and exercises you will engage in and the timeline for each one. A well-constructed agenda is essential for keeping your workshop on track and enabling you to achieve your desired outcomes.

That's why we've included a chapter in this workbook — Chapter 3: The Agenda — that outlines our suggested agenda and provides additional areas you could add based on the unique needs of your business. This chapter provides a comprehensive guide to help you develop a custom agenda that works for you and includes tips on how to guarantee that your work stays focused, relevant, and productive.

Part 3 - The Importance of Preparation

Planning and preparation are key elements to ensuring success. Without proper planning and preparation, the workshop will not yield the desire results. One of the most important steps in the preparation process is the collection of data and facts. This data will provide a foundation for the workshop and will be essential in making informed decisions during the planning meetings.

The data and facts that need to be collected before the workshop or planning starts include:

- [ ] 1. Business financial statements
- [ ] 2. Market analysis
- [ ] 3. Customer data
- [ ] 4. Staffing information
- [ ] 5. Supply chain analysis
- [ ] 6. Sales and marketing strategies
- [ ] 7. P&L analysis and reports
- [ ] 8. Cash flow analysis and reports
- [ ] 9. A recession-focused SWOT analysis
- [ ] 10. Current business strategy

Each of these areas will provide important insights into the current state of the business and the market it operates in. There may be cases when you do not have the data or you cannot easily get it. In this case, we would recommend that you take a minute and assess how important it might be to making good decisions. In most cases, if it is not easy to get, we would recommend moving on without the data. However, a few areas, like P&L, are critical. The point is to come with the best data you can, but do not spend your time trying to find it.

> *Pro Tip –* When possible, use digital forms like Microsoft Forms or Google Sheets to collect data. For example, you'll need a new SWOT from the team. Collect this using a digital form. It will make distribution and review much easier.

If you do want to collect any missing data points, there are various methods that can be used to collect this data, including conducting internal audits, market research, and data analysis.

You may choose to share this data with all participants in the planning process as a pre-read. This will give them time to understand the data and think about anything that might be important, which might be missing from the list. If you do share as a pre-read, we would strongly recommend that you make a recommendation to attendees on the minimum and maximum amount of time they should prepare for any meetings. You will find that on any team there are different personalities when it comes to prework or pre-reads. Assigning a clear amount of time they need to spend will help to eliminate the potential of someone showing up unprepared. On the other hand, team members can spend too much time preparing and overthink the process, so a maximum time is important as well.

Counter point to the pre-read concept. Amazon starts many of its meetings with a pre-read time in the meeting.[1] This is to give everyone a chance to read the information, and it also sets the expectation to not read prior to the meeting. This may or may not be right for your team, but is something to consider.

Part 4 – Who to Invite to Be Engaged in the Process

Having the right participants at your planning or recession-resistant workshop is key to ensuring its success. When planning the attendees, it's crucial to keep the number small, ideally eight people or fewer. A smaller group will lead to faster and more productive discussions. The participants should include key decision makers from your business such as:

1. Business owners
2. CEO
3. CFO
4. Other senior leaders such as HR, sales, and operations.

These individuals should have the authority to make changes in the business and should be well versed in the financial and operational aspects of the business. While departments such as IT and marketing are important, in our assessment, they are not relevant to this particular discussion.

As this process and workshop can be data heavy, it might be useful to have a business or financial analyst on standby to quickly provide any necessary information.

Choosing the right people for this work is crucial as it requires attendees who understand your company's core values and are willing to participate with a positive attitude.

Having a cross-functional team engaged and in attendance can also bring a diversity of perspectives to the table. This can lead to innovative solutions and a deeper understanding of the various challenges facing your business. These outcomes can be especially valuable during a recession, where it is crucial to think outside the box and come up with creative solutions to remain competitive.

Warning – *As the leader of the company or of the planning work, you will get pressure to bring additional individuals into the meeting. You must make the best decision on who should attend based on your organizational dynamics, and we recommend that you take them into consideration. However, the topics and discussions are very dynamic, and limiting the number of people who attend the meetings or workshops will create better outcomes.*

Part 5 – Creating a Timeline

To create a successful and productive plan, it is important to provide a comprehensive timeline for the team involved. A timeline provides structure and helps keep everyone on track, ensuring that each step of the process is completed efficiently and effectively. While the workshop can be the *Big Moment*, the plan is the most important outcome.

Having this timeline will remind the team that this is not a one-and-done event. You have a plan beyond just a meeting. This will increase their investment into the process and also make the outcome more productive.

The following are key components that should be included in the timeline:

1. **Planning** - This is the first and arguably most important step. During this phase, you should take the time to research and understand the key factors that will impact your business during a recession. This includes understanding your target market, industry trends, and the overall economic landscape.

2. **Preparing** - Gather all the materials and resources you need to execute the workshop or planning meetings. In addition, you need to create worksheets and exercises for participants, secure a location for the workshop, and set up any necessary technology.

3. **Organizing** - Determine the logistics of the workshop, such as who will be attending, what the agenda will be, and what materials will be needed. Plan out any breaks or meals during the workshop to help participants remain engaged and focused.

4. **Executing the work** - The day of the workshop is the time to put all your planning and preparation into action. The team will come together to identify data points and brainstorm strategies for making the business recession-proof.

5. **Documenting the plan** - After the planning, it's essential to document all the key takeaways and action items. This will serve as a roadmap for the team going forward and ensure that everyone is on the same page as the plan moves forward. Do NOT miss this step. It will make all the work worthless if you do not document it.

6. **Implementing the plan** - Put the strategies and action items developed during the workshop into motion, including making changes to operations, investing in new technologies, or revamping marketing strategies.

7. **Managing through the recession** - This step is ongoing and involves monitoring and adjusting the plan as necessary to help the business remain recession-proof. You may need to make changes to the plan in response to changes in the market or seek out new opportunities as they arise.

Also, it may be valuable to include regular check-ins or progress reports in the timeline. This will help the team stay accountable and make sure that everyone is working towards the same goals.

Overall, creating a comprehensive timeline is crucial for the success of the entire process and the journey of making a business recession resistant. It provides a roadmap for the team, helps to keep everyone on track, and enables each step to be completed efficiently and effectively.

> *Pro Tip – The easiest part of this process is holding a meeting or workshop. Not only is it easy, but it will create a feeling that you did something and reduce any fear or anxiety about the future. This is just a sugar rush. To get real value, ensure that you do the additional work of building, communicating, and executing a plan from the meetings you hold.*

Sample Timeline and KPIs - sample timeline for the recession-resistant workshop:

Planning Phase (Week 1-2):

- Form a team and assign roles and responsibilities.
- Identify and prioritize key areas of focus for the plan.
- Determine a realistic, but aggressive, timeline for the project.
- Establish a system for tracking progress and measuring success.

Preparation Phase (Week 3-4):

- Gather all required data and information.
- Develop a detailed agenda.
- Identify and invite stakeholders to participate in the workshop.
- Prepare all necessary materials and resources.

Organization Phase (Week 5-6):

- Finalize the agenda and schedule the workshop.
- Confirm all participants and their availability.
- Arrange for necessary logistics and support for the workshop.
- Communicate the final details to all stakeholders.

Execution Phase (Week 7-8):

- Conduct the meetings or workshop as planned.
- Facilitate productive and meaningful discussions.
- Capture all key insights and recommendations.
- Ensure all participants are engaged and involved.

Documentation Phase (Week 9-10):

- Document all proceedings and outcomes.
- Develop a comprehensive action plan based on the results.
- Share the action plan with all stakeholders and gather feedback.
- Revise and finalize the action plan.

Implementation Phase (Week 11-12):

- Begin implementing the action plan.
- Assign tasks and responsibilities to team members.
- Establish regular check-ins and progress updates.
- Track and measure the results of the action plan.

Management Phase (Ongoing):

- Continuously monitor and assess the impact of the action plan.
- Identify and address any challenges or roadblocks.
- Make necessary adjustments to the action plan as needed.
- Report on the progress and impact of the action plan.

Key Performance Indicators (KPIs) to track:

- Completion of each phase within the timeline.
- Number of participants and their level of engagement.
- Quality and effectiveness of the proceedings.
- Adherence to budget and resource constraints.
- Success and impact of implementing the action plan.

By tracking these KPIs, the team will be able to make certain that the timeline is on track and that the workshop is delivering the desired results. Also, by regularly monitoring and assessing the impact of the action plan, the team will be able to make necessary adjustments and continue to drive value for the company during and after the recession.

EXERCISE 3
www.growprofitordie.com

GROW PROFIT OR DIE

After reading about the timeline, take a few minutes to create your timeline for preparing for a recession.
What actions should you take for each phase?
What additional steps do you need to create a realistic timeline?

STEPS	# Weeks Or Days
1	
2	
3	
4	
5	
6	
7	
8	

Part 6 - Tools

The use of online and physical tools for the Recession-Resistant Workshop can drastically enhance the efficiency and productivity of the session. These tools foster effective communication, encourage collaboration, facilitate creative brainstorming, and allow for comprehensive documentation and progress tracking.

Online Tools

1. **Miro**

    Miro is a virtual whiteboard platform that encourages team collaboration, and we cannot overstate the importance of this tool. It will take a little time to master. However, whatever time you invest in mastering it will be paid back in the increased collaboration capabilities that it provides for you.

    - **Brainstorming and Mind-Mapping:** Miro's extensive canvas allows the entire team to participate in brainstorming sessions concurrently. It facilitates visual idea mapping, which encourages creativity and improves problem-solving capabilities.

    - **Planning and Polling:** With Miro, thoughts can be organized, timelines plotted, to-do lists created, and tasks prioritized. It serves as a shared workspace to outline the action plan and strategy during the workshop. You can also use the tool to poll the team and get votes on topics.

    - **Documenting and Sharing:** Miro allows for real-time documentation of all ideas and decisions made during the workshop. These boards can be easily shared among participants, enabling everyone to have the same information.

2. **OneNote**

   OneNote is a digital note-taking app from Microsoft that can prove highly valuable in a workshop setting.

   - **Note-taking:** Participants can take detailed notes during the workshop, including text, images, audio, and even video. Notes can be organized into sections and pages for easy navigation.

   - **Collaboration:** OneNote allows multiple users to work on a single notebook, making it an excellent tool for collaboration. Users can see who made specific changes and when, fostering transparency and teamwork.

   - **Integration:** Being a part of the Microsoft suite, OneNote integrates well with other Microsoft applications like Word, Excel, PowerPoint, and Forms, which can enhance the workshop experience.

3. **Microsoft Forms**

   Microsoft Forms is a simple, lightweight tool that allows you to create surveys, quizzes, and polls.

   - **Feedback Collection:** Using Microsoft Forms, you can create post-workshop feedback forms. This can help in understanding what worked well and what needs improvement.

   - **Quizzes and Polls:** To increase engagement and ensure understanding of the concepts discussed, you can create quizzes and polls. These can be filled in real-time, and the responses can be seen immediately.

Physical Tools

1. **Whiteboard and Markers:** A physical whiteboard can also be useful in a face-to-face workshop setting for brainstorming, idea visualization, and for participants to take down key points. Have markers in various colors for participants to use.

2. **Post-it Notes:** These are great for brainstorming sessions and voting or prioritizing ideas. Participants can write their thoughts or suggestions on these and stick them on the whiteboard.

3. **Notebooks and Pens:** Personal notebooks can be used by participants for jotting down notes, thoughts, or questions that they may have during the workshop.

4. **Timer:** A timer can be used to make certain the workshop stays on schedule. This is especially important during activities or breakout sessions to improve time efficiency.

The combination of these online and physical tools can substantially enhance the effectiveness of your meeting. They will improve communication, facilitate collaboration, foster creativity, and ensure that all ideas and decisions are thoroughly documented and organized.

Part 7 - Wrap Up

In this chapter, we covered the essential steps to take when planning for a recession and a potential recession-resistant workshop. First, preparation and planning are crucial to the success of the meeting, and it is essential to collect data and facts relevant to your business before the work begins. This data will help you make informed decisions and make certain the time invested is productive. Second, it is important to invite the right participants to the meetings — including key decision-makers, business leaders, and a cross-functional team — to bring a diversity of perspectives to the discussion. The ideal group size is six people with a maximum of eight. It is crucial to choose participants who understand your company's core values and are willing to participate with a positive attitude. By following the guidance and advice in this chapter, you will be well on your way to planning a successful recession-resistant workshop for your business.

Summary of Chapter:

This chapter focuses on preparing your business for a potential recession. Key points include:

1. Planning your meetings or workshop: Confirm that you have the right resources and approach in place to achieve desired outcomes.

2. Importance of an agenda: Develop a custom agenda tailored to your business needs to keep the process on track and productive.

3. Importance of preparation: Collect crucial data and information to make informed decisions during the meetings.

4. Who to invite: Include key decision-makers from your business, such as business owners, CEO, CFO, and other senior leaders, to help provide a successful outcome.

5. Creating a timeline: Develop a comprehensive timeline to provide structure and keep the team on track.

By following these guidelines, you can plan and execute a workshop to help your business navigate a potential recession and position it for success.

Task List for This Chapter:

- [ ] 1. Form a planning team and assign roles and responsibilities.

- [ ] 2. Identify and prioritize key areas of focus for the plan.

- [ ] 3. Develop a detailed agenda tailored to your business needs.

- [ ] 4. Gather relevant data and information, such as financial statements, market analysis, and staffing information.

- [ ] 5. Share the collected data with participants as a pre-read.

- [ ] 6. Identify and invite key decision-makers from your business to participate in the process.

- [ ] 7. Consider having a business or financial analyst available for quick data access during the meetings.

- [ ] 8. Create a comprehensive timeline, including planning, preparation, organization, execution, documentation, implementation, and management phases.

- [ ] 9. Secure a location for the workshop and set up necessary technology.

- [ ] 10. Plan breaks and meals during the workshop to keep participants engaged and focused.

☐ 11. Document key takeaways and action items.

☐ 12. Implement the strategies and action items.

☐ 13. Monitor and adjust the plan as necessary, with regular check-ins or progress reports.

☐ 14. Track Key Performance Indicators (KPIs) to ensure success and impact on the business.

Chapter 2 – Preparation

Part 1 - Overview

In this chapter, we aim to provide guidance on the importance of gathering key data and information. The information you gather will help you plan for the future and increase the value and robustness of your team's planning. The purpose of this chapter is to equip participants with the necessary facts and data to make informed decisions and develop a comprehensive recession-resistant plan. However you intend to plan for the future, these are the key areas to gather.

We strongly recommend that participants gather data and information in the following 10 areas:

- Business financial statements
- Market analysis
- Customer data
- Staffing information
- Supply chain analysis
- Sales and marketing strategies
- P&L analysis and reports

- Cash flow analysis and reports
- Recession-focused SWOT analysis
- Business strategy

Although we strongly recommend these 10 areas, participants should still gather whatever they believe to be the most important data and information. However, covering these 10 areas will provide a comprehensive view of the business and the current market conditions, which will lead to a well-informed team.

We will go into each of these areas in more detail later in this chapter, but for now, we wanted to provide a high-level overview of the key data and information that participants should gather to have a successful outcome. The objective is to provide participants with the necessary materials to make informed decisions and develop a robust and effective recession-resistant plan.

Part 2 - Areas to Prepare

Business Financial Statements: When it comes to preparing for a potential recession, it's important to have a thorough understanding of your business's financial position. The CEO and CFO should work together to gather the most relevant financial statements that accurately reflect the current and past performance of the business. These statements will provide a snapshot of the business's financial health and can help identify areas that may need attention to better weather an economic downturn.

In general, the following financial statements are recommended:

1. **Balance Sheet:** A balance sheet provides a snapshot of the business's assets, liabilities, and equity as of a specific date. This statement can help identify areas where the business may be overleveraged and in need of attention.

2. **Income Statement:** An income statement provides information on the business's revenue, expenses, and profit over a specified period of time. This statement can help identify areas where the business may be spending too much or not generating enough revenue.

3. **Cash Flow Statement:** A cash flow statement provides information on the inflows and outflows of cash for a specified period of time. This statement is important for businesses because it can help identify potential cash flow problems and help the business plan for future expenses.

Important – *Cash flow is arguably the most important thing a business needs to watch in good times and during any downturn. In a recession, most businesses will say, "We don't even want to look at cash flow." I'm not sure why most business leaders don't want to track this, but I believe it is similar to Schrödinger's Cat. Just like the cat, if I don't look, it's neither dead nor alive. It's a great way to think about quantum physics, but NOT your cash flow. You need to be tracking this and looking at it.*

4. Optional - Statement of Retained Earnings: This statement provides information on the business's retained earnings over a specified period of time. This statement is essential for businesses because it can help the business plan for future expenditures and investments.

In addition to these financial statements, the business may also want to consider tracking certain financial key performance indicators (KPIs), such as profit margins, return on investment (ROI), and net operating income (NOI). These KPIs can provide valuable insights into the business's financial performance and help identify areas where the business may need to focus its efforts.

Remember, the financial statements and KPIs that are most important for a business will depend on its specific circumstances and goals. Businesses should consult with their CPA or accounting firm to determine which financial statements to use.

> *Pro Tip – Most industries have either a trade association or standards organization that can give them guidelines for what are the best practices and measurements for their specific organization.*
>
> *These associations and organizations will also typically provide round tables or forums for noncompetitive businesses in your space to support each other. This is a great area to look for support in financial measurements. If you have not had access to this type of information, do this immediately. See Chapter 31 in* **Wake-Up Call** *on the power and importance of community.*

EXERCISE 4
www.growprofitordie.com

GROW PROFIT OR DIE

What Are the Top 5 Areas Your Team Needs to Prepare For?

Now that you have reviewed the areas we recommend to prepare for a recession, take a minute and document the areas that are most important to review.

Start with your top five, and list the reasons you think they are important. It will help you focus on getting the most important items accomplished.

Area	Reason
1 _____	_____
2 _____	_____
3 _____	_____
4 _____	_____
5 _____	_____

Positive Point – By maintaining a firm grip on your finances during a recession, you will be in an optimum position to take advantage of good bargains on businesses. A crucial reason to maintain a firm grip on your finances during a recession is the availability of deals. If you weather the recession with minimal impact and have cash on hand, it will be an opportune time to invest because everything will be at a discount. See Chapter 34 in Wake-Up Call, which is entitled "Sharks Are in the Water" for more information on this topic.

Part 3 - Market Analysis

Market analysis is a crucial aspect of preparing for a potential recession as it provides insight into the current and future trends of the market. It helps businesses understand their competition, **customer preferences**, market opportunities, and potential risks. Some of the key data points to gather for market analysis are:

1. **Industry trends and reports**: This includes reports from industry associations, research firms, and government agencies. These reports provide a comprehensive overview of the industry, including growth rates, market size, and trends.

2. **Customer data:** Understanding customer preferences, buying habits, and behavior is crucial for market analysis. This data can be collected through customer surveys, market research, and data analytics.

Important – *One of the areas we believe your business can have the greatest return on effort is to focus on your **core customer**. We have a section dedicated to that concept, and this research will be critical in this area.*

3. **Competitor analysis:** Analyzing the competition is important in order to understand their strengths, weaknesses, and strategies. This information can be gathered through examining competitor websites, financial statements, and market research.

4. **Market demographics:** Demographic information such as age, gender, income, and education levels can help businesses understand their target market and make informed decisions.

5. **Economic indicators:** Economic indicators such as inflation, unemployment rates, and Gross Domestic Product (GDP) can provide insight into the overall health of the economy and help businesses make informed decisions.

Pro Tip – This data on economic indicators is free from our government and is readily available. Unfortunately, most of us don't monitor it, and more importantly, we don't know how it affects our business.

6. **Sales and revenue data:** Sales and revenue data can provide a clear picture of the current market demand for your particular product or service.

> *Pro Tip – Sales Concept – It has been our observation that humans have a defense mechanism we use when we see bad news. We will lie to ourselves or rationalize negative data or facts. In some parts of life, this can be a positive human trait. However, when managing your sales pipeline/forecast, you must combat this urge. In the lead up to and during the recession, you will be looking for silver linings. If they are real, embrace them. Just please don't make them up, and don't let your team fall for them.*

In addition to these data points, it's also important to consider key performance indicators (KPIs) such as market share, customer satisfaction, and brand recognition.

To gather this data, businesses can conduct market research, utilize data analytics tools, and engage with industry experts and market research firms. Be sure to engage your marketing team as they should have this data. If they do not, this would be a key KPI for them in the future. It is ok to let sales in on the discussion, but be very careful with how much you rely on their *facts*, because they are mostly opinion. Plus, they are there to support their agenda, which is typically achieving quota.

If you need more help in the gathering information, here are some suggestions on other areas to examine. Gathering relevant data and information can help businesses better understand their target market, competition, and potential risks and opportunities. There are several ways to gather information for market analysis:

1. **Market Research:** This involves collecting data through surveys, focus groups, and other research methods to gain insights into customer needs, preferences, and behaviors. Market research can also help businesses understand their target market demographics and size.

2. **Data Analytics Tools:** These tools can provide valuable data on consumer behavior, market trends, and competitor activities. Some popular data analytics tools include Google Analytics, SEMRush, and Moz.

3. **Industry Experts and Market Research Firms:** Engaging with industry experts and market research firms can provide businesses with access to data, insights, and expertise that would be difficult to gather on their own. These experts can also provide a valuable outside perspective that can help businesses make informed decisions.

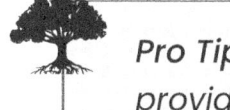

> *Pro Tip – Some companies that want your business might provide you with free data for the opportunity to do business with your company. In many cases they have gathered the data to give it away. We recommend seeing what is available prior to doing the work yourself or paying for it.*

4. **Marketing Team:** The marketing team can be an excellent resource for gathering information on market trends, consumer behavior, and competitor activities. They should be able to provide insights into the target market and any potential risks or opportunities that may impact the business.

5. **AI Tools:** As of the writing of this book in 2024, there has been an increase in the availability of AI tools, such as ChatGPT. They are an important tool for doing this research and even for rendering an opinion. It can NOT be overstated; use these tools.

Short Cut – Use AI tools such as ChatGPT.

The human capacity for pattern recognition and intuitive decision-making is genuine and powerful. Our subconscious mind consistently searches for patterns, suggesting potential choices based on our past experiences. When you've spent years in your business, it becomes increasingly vital to balance your gut instincts with research findings. Both should be regarded as significant contributors to your decision-making process. Neither should be relied upon exclusively, nor should either be disregarded. Remember, your intuition, shaped by your accumulated experiences, can be a more formidable tool than you might imagine.

Part 4 - Customer Data

Customer data is a crucial aspect of understanding a business's strengths, weaknesses, and opportunities in the market. Keep in mind that this data is critical for the section on *core customer* that the team will be reviewing. To gather meaningful customer data, it's important to consider the following:

1. **Customer Segmentation:** Knowing your core customer, who makes up your target market, and their demographic and psychographic profiles will help you understand their buying habits and preferences. This information can be collected through surveys, focus groups, and market research.

2. **Sales Data:** The sales team is a valuable resource for customer data, as they have direct interaction with customers and can provide insight into what is working and what is not. However, it's important to not rely solely on the sales team, as their perspective may be biased. Sales teams will often guide the discussion/discovery for what will work for them.

   Caution – Be cautious when engaging the sales team in this process. Remember, you hired them because they are good at convincing people to do things, including you.

3. **Customer Feedback:** Customer feedback can provide valuable information about their experiences, expectations, and perceptions of your business. This can be collected through surveys, customer service interactions, and online reviews. **If you do not have this data, build a simple Microsoft form, and get that data NOW. This is one of the most critical data points you need for your business.**

4. **CRM Systems:** A Customer Relationship Management (CRM) system can provide a wealth of customer data, including purchase history, contact information, and engagement metrics. If your business does not currently have a CRM system, consider implementing one as it can greatly aid in collecting, organizing, and analyzing customer data.

Critical Point – If you do not have a CRM system, this is an immediate add to your company. It would be the equivalent of not having a financial system and only using Excel to manage your finances. Get a CRM solution today. HubSpot has a great option for small businesses if cost is a hindrance.

5. **Customer Data Analysis:** It's important to note that the top 80% of revenue-generating customers should be a focus of the customer data analysis. Understanding the characteristics and habits of these customers will be vital in formulating a strategy for a potential recession.

Critical Point – In most businesses the 80/20 rule applies; 20% of your customers will make up 80% of your revenue. Are you focused on them?

6. **Gathering Customer Data:** When gathering customer data, it's important to involve stakeholders from different departments — including the sales, marketing, and customer service teams — to ensure a well-rounded understanding of the customers and their needs.

7. **AI Tools:** Analyze customer data and trends with AI, which has access to a considerable amount of data. Do not leave out AI.

The customer data will be critical during your planning or workshop. This book will guide you through using this data. The goal will be to help you discover and better understand your *core customer*.

Part 5 - Staffing Information

In the world of business, having a clear understanding of your workforce is crucial. In preparation for a potential recession, it's imperative to gather staffing information and HR data to help inform your decisions. Here are a few key areas to focus on when collecting this information:

1. **Employee headcount:** Have a clear understanding of your current headcount. This will help you make informed decisions about layoffs or restructuring. Your HR system or payroll reports can provide this data.

2. **Department staffing levels:** It's important to understand the minimum staffing levels in each department so you can determine which departments may be most affected by layoffs or restructuring. You can get this information from HR or department managers.

> *Pro Tip – Do not skip this step. Some managers are significantly weaker at managing employee efficiency and head count. It is almost guaranteed you have more people than you need to run your business today.x To prepare for a recession, you must have detailed information on your staffing levels. This will be crucial information for your business, and it will help you identify which departments need to address staffing concerns.*

3. **Employee performance data:** When you are faced with making decisions regarding layoffs or restructuring, performance data on each employee will enable you to make a well-informed decision.

4. **Third-party payroll data:** If your business uses a third-party payroll company, it's important to gather data from them as well. This information can provide a more comprehensive picture of your workforce. Many of these systems have robust reports you have likely never seen. It is important to push your HR manager to find and deliver them to you.

5. **Employee engagement data:** Employee engagement data can help you understand the morale of your workforce, which can inform decisions. You can get this information through employee surveys or through HR metrics.

It's important to engage your HR team and department managers when gathering staffing information. Having a comprehensive understanding of your workforce will help you. Also, if your business does not have an HR system in place, consider implementing one prior to a potential recession to help you gather and track this important data.

> *Pro Tip – It is never fun to talk about or even research the people part of this work. It means someone could be negatively affected by your actions, and that's not fun. Regrettably, you are paying for the sins of the past here. Most organizations do not practice discipline or restraint during the good times. Much like biological entities, they grow to fit the size of their environment. In this context, businesses spend their profits hiring people and growing, when really, they do not need the additional workforce. As in life, you will need to change this. Do yourself a favor and ensure the company applies the appropriate discipline in the future, so you don't have to go through this again.*

Part 6 - Supply Chain

When it comes to gathering information for a supply chain analysis, it's important to have a comprehensive understanding of the following information for the company:

- Suppliers
- Inventory levels
- Delivery timelines
- Potential disruptions

This information can help the company prepare for any potential supply chain disruptions during a recession.

Once the company has a good understanding of its supply chain, it's time to gather data and analyze it. This can be done through a variety of methods, including conducting a supplier survey, reviewing inventory levels, and analyzing delivery times. The company can also work with industry experts or third-party consultants to gather information and analyze the data.

Finally, it's important to remember that a supply chain is a living and dynamic component of a business, so it's important to regularly review and update the information gathered for a supply chain analysis. This will help the company stay ahead of potential supply chain disruptions and ensure that it is well-prepared for a potential recession.

Observation – For 30 plus years, America practiced the just-in-time manufacturing model, an incredible tool that shortened inventory needs and freed up cash. In our opinion, this was one of the major factors that enabled America to continue to grow, even with global pressures. The concept bled into most American businesses and is not just a manufacturing practice. During COVID-19, we saw a breakdown of the supply chain and the breakdown of just-in-time manufacturing.

In parallel, we saw balance sheets balloon with cash in some businesses, thanks to many factors. As a result, many organizations that we have worked with are fat with inventory, and some of the past discipline of just-in-time has been eroded or is entirely gone. This is a major stressor on cash flow, and we do not believe businesses in America have really seen the full impact of this change. When a downturn or recession hits, this will be one of the first and major issues. You will give anything to NOT have that inventory and to have cash on hand. This makes this section critical.

After the COVID-19 supply chain issues, many businesses started carrying extra inventory. In a possible recession, this inventory could become a write off, if business slows. When you consider the loss of cash due to excess inventory and the possible write off, it becomes a double whammy.

Part 7 - Sales and Marketing Strategy

Warning – This section is somewhat of a repeat from earlier material, from a different lens. We feel it is still important to go through the exercise below.

The current sales and marketing strategies of a company play a crucial role in its success, especially during a potential recession. It is imperative to gather information on the company's existing sales and marketing strategies in preparation for the planning meetings or recession-resistant workshop. A formal sales process or strategy provides clarity and direction in the sales process, making it easier to measure and report on key performance indicators (KPIs) during the recession.

In many of our engagements, we find that most companies under $100M in revenue per year do not have a sales process or play book. Similar to our comments on CRM, you need to get this now. No company should run without this, no matter the size.
Contact Red Wagon for help at wade@redwagonadvisors.com!

In case the company lacks a formal sales process or strategy, invest in creating one. Read Jack Daly's book, *Hyper Sales Growth*[1], and work with a firm like Red Wagon Advisors if you lack a formal sales process. A sales strategy or playbook is especially important in a recession as it helps the sales team stay focused and on track even in stressful times.

To gather information on the current sales and marketing strategies, the sales team should be involved in the process as they have a wealth of knowledge about the sales process and strategies being used. Providing them with clear directions and a timeline will help guarantee that the information is gathered in a timely and efficient manner. While it is important to aim for complete and accurate information, anything is better than nothing. The most critical information to gather is how sales reporting and KPIs are currently recorded and tracked.

Come to these meetings with the current commission structure in hand to assess if any adjustments need to be made. Recessions can be a great time to realign compensation that may have gotten out of balance.

Finally, it is important to present the information in a clear and concise manner during your meetings. Data visualization tools such as graphs, charts, and tables can help make the information easier to understand and will help you make informed decisions. A well-presented report will keep the process focused and productive, allowing the team to effectively prepare for a potential recession.

EXERCISE 5
www.growprofitordie.com

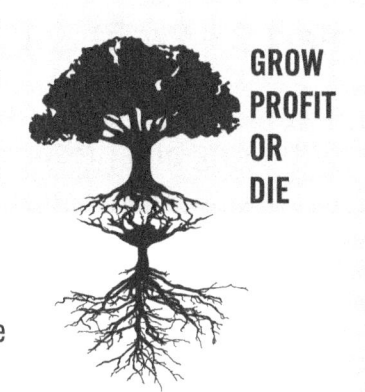

Sales/Marketing Playbook

The sales and marketing process/playbook is one of the most difficult items to manage and maintain.

What are the top areas that need inspection and possible correction?

Area	Challenge
1	
2	
3	
4	
5	
6	
7	

Part 8 - Profit and Loss

Gathering and presenting a Profit and Loss (P&L) statement is a typical component of preparing for a potential recession. This is a normal and default task that is done on a regular basis in any company. Since that is the case, let's make sure to ask for additional rigor or seriousness when gathering the P&L statement for this activity. Ask, "What have we taken for granted in the past," or "is there anything we would do differently if time permitted it in the P&L?"

> *Pro Tip –* The person who handles financial tasks in your business is almost always territorial. They will ask a lot of questions and encourage you do to this their way. In principle, we support letting the financial people do their job and not getting in their way. However, in this situation, you need to lean in and not be guided by them. We will stop short of labeling all CFOs control freaks, but we think you get the picture.
> P.S. If there is any fraud in your company, this would uncover it. So, if your Spidey senses tingle, don't ignore them. You might find a bigger problem while working on a future issue.

To gather the necessary information for a P&L statement, it is recommended that you work closely with the company's financial department or with a trusted accountant or CPA. The financial department or accountant will have the necessary experience and expertise to guarantee the accuracy and completeness of the information. They should also be able to provide historical P&L statements to help identify trends and patterns.

When preparing the P&L statement, make sure you have a clear and concise format. The statement should include revenue, cost of goods sold, gross profit, operating expenses, and net income. It is also important to consider adding additional details, such as departmental expenses, to provide a more comprehensive view of the company's financial performance.

In presenting the P&L statement, use data visualization tools such as graphs, charts, and tables. This makes the information easier to understand and provides a clear picture of the company's financial performance. Also, provide context and explanation for any variances in the data, such as changes in revenue or expenses.

Part 9 - Cash Flow Analysis and Reports

Cash flow . . . This can be tricky. In many companies there is not strong cash flow reporting or management. People also wonder, "What is good cash flow, and what tools should we use to monitor it?" Some people consider their equity as an indicator of good cash flow, while others see low bank debt as a key measure of success. Do not get caught up in getting this right. Get caught up in getting started. Your cash flow is a lifetime exercise that never ends, and you will always be getting better. Just get started, and remember few businesses even measure it, let alone manage it.

In the Scaling Up family of products, we have several tools to help with managing and reporting on cash flow. We will suggest a few here and would welcome a chance to meet with you and explore the subject more thoroughly.

It is important to involve the CFO, CEO, and accounting team in the process of gathering and analyzing the cash flow reports. They will have the expertise and knowledge to ensure that the data is accurate and presented in a format that is easy to understand. Just like the P & L statement, the presentation of the cash flow analysis and reports should be clear and concise, using graphs, charts, and tables to help the team visualize the data.

When evaluating cash flow, encourage the planning team to discuss their gut feelings on the topic. This allows for healthy dialogue and encourages open communication about the company's current financial situation. By involving all team members, you will have a better understanding of their perspectives and potential biases. Encouraging honest discussion about the cash flow will ensure that everyone is on the same page and working towards the same goal. This will create a stronger foundation and lead to more productive and meaningful conversations.

When presenting the cash flow information during any of your planning sessions, it is important to focus on key performance indicators such as

- Operating cash flow
- Net cash flow
- Free cash flow

These metrics will give the team a clear understanding of the company's ability to generate cash and pay its bills. This data will help you make informed decisions as you prepare for a potential recession.

In summary, to prepare for these planning meetings, gather an accurate and up-to-date cash flow analysis, along with other reports. While cashflow is one of the most difficult and frustrating areas to engage in, this process is critical. Take it seriously.

Part 10 - Recession-Focused SWOT Analysis

For the recession-focused SWOT analysis, gather input from each of the participants in the planning. This will provide a well-rounded perspective on the strengths, weaknesses, opportunities, and threats facing the business in the event of a recession. To glean this information, use a digital tool such as Microsoft Forms, which makes it easier to consolidate and share the data.

Before conducting the SWOT analysis, instruct the staff on creating the analysis with a **recession focus in mind**. This means that they should consider the potential impacts of a recession on the business and think about how it could affect each area of the SWOT analysis.

Once the staff has completed the SWOT analysis, consolidate the results and look for any themes. This will help the team see where they have commonalities and where they may have differing opinions, which can be valuable in creating an in-depth discussion during the workshop.

We recommend appointing a designated person to consolidate the SWOT results from the staff prior to the in-person meeting. This person should be organized and detail-oriented, as the consolidation process can be time-consuming and requires attention to detail.

Your team may surprise you with not only great answers, but also robust data. If you feel there is enough data, we recommend having AI tools analyze it for you to determine patterns and even make recommendations. Doing this can add an additional lens to the conversation.

> **Pro Tip –** If you have the time, have a larger number of people take the SWOT analysis. This will give you a broader viewpoint of the business and provide the basis for a more thorough discussion. Again, you could use AI or ChatGPT to help you consolidate the results.

Part 11 - Business Strategy

Gather existing business strategy documents. Before the planning workshop, collect all relevant strategy documents, goals, and one-page plans. This will provide a foundation for the work you will be doing, allowing the team to review, tweak and strengthen the existing strategy in preparation for a potential recession.

To gather these documents, start by identifying who within the organization would have access to them. This could be the CEO, COO, CFO, or HR manager. Once identified, reach out to these individuals and request that they bring updated versions of any relevant strategy documents to the session.

Do not forget to consider any third-party providers who may have a role in your organization's strategy. For example, if you have a consulting firm, they may have created a strategy document for your organization. Be sure to include them in the process of gathering these documents, and make sure they can provide updated versions of any relevant documents.

In preparation for the in-person meeting, review and consolidate these documents into a single location, such as a shared folder or document management system. This will make it easier for the team to access and review the documents during the working sessions.

> *Pro Tip* – *If you have or had an existing one-page plan, be sure to review and focus on that. The fact that you have this document and that it is part of your normal business practices will help you prepare any recession-readiness documents or tools. So, dust off that old one-page plan, and make sure it is up to date or get it up to date as part of this process.*

Finally, it is vital to remember that your focus is to assemble existing strategy documents. The goal is not to create new strategy documents. By doing so, the team will be able to identify areas for improvement and work together to create a stronger, more resilient strategy in preparation for a potential recession.

Part 12- Wrap Up

Preparing for a recession-resistant workshop is a critical component in ensuring the success of your recession plan. By gathering and analyzing the right data, businesses can make informed decisions and create a comprehensive plan to prepare for a potential recession.

It is also important to be ready to review and update existing business strategy documents. This will allow for a more informed and strategic discussion and help identify areas for improvement.

"Remember, the more work you put into the preparation, the more value you will get from the workshop."

Adequate preparation will help guarantee a productive and valuable experience for all participants. By working together, businesses can create a comprehensive and effective plan to weather any future recession.

EXERCISE 6
www.growprofitordie.com

GROW PROFIT OR DIE

What part of your current strategy gives you pause or is not working?

What is your strategy?

Can you go into a recession excited about your strategy?

Why or Why Not?

What Should You Fix?

Summary of Chapter:

Chapter 2 of the book focuses on the importance of gathering key data and information in preparation for a recession-resistant workshop. This data will help participants make informed decisions and develop a comprehensive plan to withstand an economic downturn. The chapter outlines ten areas to focus on:

1. Business financial statements

2. Market analysis

3. Customer data

4. Staffing information

5. Supply chain analysis

6. Sales and marketing strategies

7. P&L analysis and reports

8. Cash flow analysis and reports

9. Recession-focused SWOT analysis

10. Business Strategy

Participants should collect information in these areas to ensure a successful workshop. This chapter provides a detailed explanation of each area and the information that should be collected. By covering these ten areas, participants will gain a comprehensive understanding of the business and market conditions, enabling them to create a well-informed and effective recession-resistant plan.

Task List for This Chapter:

☐ 1. **Gather business financial statements:** Balance sheet, income statement, cash flow statement.

☐ 2. **Conduct market analysis:** Market trends, competitor analysis, customer preferences, potential risks.

☐ 3. **Collect customer data:** Demographics, buying patterns, customer satisfaction.

☐ 4. **Assemble staffing information:** Employee headcount, department staffing levels, employee performance data, third-party payroll data.

☐ 5. **Analyze the supply chain:** Identify key suppliers and products/services, assess inventory levels and delivery times, evaluate potential disruptions.

☐ 6. **Review sales and marketing strategies:** Sales processes and KPIs, marketing strategies, commission structure.

- [ ] **7. Prepare P&L analysis and reports:** Revenue, expenses, profit, departmental expenses, cash flow statement and balance sheet.

- [ ] **8. Conduct cash flow analysis and reports:** Review financial statements, utilize financial software or tools.

- [ ] **9. Complete recession-focused SWOT analysis:** Gather input from all participantsonsolidate and analyze the results.

- [ ] **10. Collect business strategy documents:** Existing strategy documents, goals and one-page plans.

Chapter 3 – The Agenda

The purpose of this chapter is to guide you in creating the agenda for your recession-resistant planning. A well-planned agenda is crucial in ensuring that whatever you do — either planning meetings or a workshop — is productive, efficient, and effective. This chapter will provide you with guidelines on what content to include, how to prioritize it, and how to avoid overloading the agenda.

We have provided a suggested agenda for your reference, but feel free to edit it to fit your specific needs. Keep in mind that the content of the agenda should be relevant to the goals and objectives of the business and be structured in a way that allows for a smooth flow of information and discussion.

Remember, that the agenda should serve as a road map for the planning meetings or workshop and be flexible enough to accommodate changes and unexpected developments. This chapter will provide you with tips and best practices for creating an effective agenda that will keep your team focused and on track. By following these guidelines, you will be able to create an agenda that sets the stage for a successful recession-resistant workshop.

> *Pro Tip –* *We have found that when building the agenda, the leader will try to put too much on it. Resist that urge. If you publish the agenda, people will follow it. However, they will begin to discount the process if they see that you are not staying with the agenda or on time. Create an agenda you know you can achieve, and add to it if you have extra time. Take it from us. We have done hundreds of all-day events.*

Part 1 - Start with Reviewing our Agenda

Before diving into creating the agenda, it is important to first review the suggested agenda provided. This agenda was created for a company with $50,000,000-a-year in revenue and 200 employees. So it may need to be adjusted to fit your specific business needs.

While we encourage you to have a full-day workshop, many of you may want to split the activities in this book into several planning meetings. There may also be people who use the book as a planning guide and do the work on their own. Whatever way you choose, the agenda will be a critical guide to determining and completing the necessary tasks.

As you review the agenda, make a list of the key outcomes you hope to achieve. The final agenda should cover all the important topics and address the specific needs of your business. We even suggest publishing those key outcomes, so the team knows what they are working towards. There is really no reason to keep that a secret.

Keep in mind the format of the suggested agenda, but also consider any changes that need to be made to fit the unique requirements of your business. This could include adding or removing certain topics, adjusting the order of the agenda items, or allowing more time for certain discussions. Remember, you may try to do too much. So, be very careful adding to the agenda.

Overall, the goal is to create an agenda that is tailored to your business and will help you effectively prepare for a potential recession.

On the next page, you will find the agenda for you to review. On the agenda we list what we believe are potential areas you might want to include.

Sample Agenda

- Introduction and Overview of the Day
- Recession War Game
- Assumptions and Core Customer
- Lunch
- Staff Assessment
- P&L Analysis
- Cash Flow
- War Room and the Plan
- Wrap-Up and Additional Tasks

Now that you have reviewed our suggested agenda, you will want to read through the following paragraphs outlining why each component of the agenda is important. In a future chapter, we go deeper into each component, so this is just an overview.

Introduction and Overview of the Day: A successful planning meeting must start with an introduction and call to action. This sets the tone for the day and prepares participants for what is to come. The overview of the day should provide a clear picture of the schedule and what will be covered.

Recession War Game: The purpose of this agenda item is to walk the team through the financial, sales, and people challenge of a 6-to-12-month recession. It is important to *play out* the recession as a way of preparing for the discussion and debates that will arise throughout the day. This is a critical component of the planning and should not be skipped. You are doing a *rehearsal* for the coming recession. However, we recommend having a trained facilitator to lead this section.

Assumptions and Core Customers: Assumptions and core customers are critical components of any business strategy, especially in a recession. This section will help the team to identify what their assumptions are and reach a consensus on who their core customers are. Without these two pieces of information, the team will be flying blind and won't know which customer to target

Staff Assessment: Staffing is a critical component of any business, and it is important to have a clear understanding of what the company's plans are for staffing during a recession. This section will help the team to assess their current staffing situation and determine what changes, if any, need to be made.

P&L Analysis: During a recession, teams look for ways to cut costs. Reviewing the P&L with a recession mindset is critical for making informed decisions about where to cut spending. This is a rare exercise, but it is important to prepare for a recession.

Cash Flow: Cash flow is a critical component of any business, especially during a recession. This section will help the team to understand how they will manage cash flow, where it will come from, and what their philosophy is for managing it when things get tight. A trained facilitator can be helpful for discussing this topic in the workshop.

War Room and the Plan: This section focuses on creating a plan and provides follow-up from the day's work. After a full day of discussions about a potential recession, this is where the team becomes recession resistant by creating a plan for their business. This activity should not be skipped as it is important to have a clear plan in place.

Wrap Up and Additional Tasks: A successful workshop must end with a wrap-up and call to action. This chapter will provide participants with a summary of the day's events and any additional tasks that need to be completed.

Part 2 – Additional Agenda Items

What other items might be appropriate for your agenda? We will list additional topics in this section. While the time you have may not be enough to cover all these topics in depth, it is important to keep them in mind when preparing for a potential recession. Depending on your specific needs, you may choose to expand the workshop, swap out a less important topic for a more crucial one, or continue the work in smaller meetings over the next few months.

Please take a few minutes to review the items listed below and see if there is anything you would like to add or remove.

Pricing: In this session, participants will delve into their current pricing strategy and how it may need to change during a recession. They will explore pricing techniques to help them stay competitive and profitable during economic downturns.

Strategy: Participants will examine their existing strategy and make any necessary adjustments to ensure its resilience in a recession.

Decision Making and Seat of Power: This session will look at decision-making processes and examine who holds the power to make those decisions in the company. Participants will learn how to make effective decisions during a recession, who should be involved, and what kind of input is required from different teams.

Things we WON'T Do, and Things we WILL Do: This session will help participants identify the actions they need to avoid during a recession, as well as the actions they must take to protect their business. They will develop a clear plan for what they will and won't do in a recession.

Sales Team Management: This session will examine the role of the sales team in a recession. Participants will explore how to manage their sales team effectively, how to motivate them, and how to measure their performance.

Your Personal and Business Calendar: This session will help participants understand the importance of having a clear calendar of personal and business activities during a recession. Participants will explore how to prioritize activities, how to schedule necessary meetings, and how to create a routine that will help them stay on track, and NOT *stay* busy.

How We Measure Opportunities and Act on Them: This session will help participants learn how to measure opportunities and act on them effectively. They will learn about the importance of monitoring key metrics, how to track progress, and how to use data to make informed decisions.

Additional People Assessment: In this session, participants will review the existing team and have hard conversations now, as opposed to during the recession.

Supply Chain Management: Review your current suppliers and explore alternative sources for critical products and services.

Leadership and Communication: Examine how your leadership style and communication strategies can impact your business during a recession.

Additional P&L Work Cost: Cutting costs and resource optimization - Identify areas where costs can be reduced and resources reallocated to maximize efficiency and maintain profitability.

Business Networking and Collaboration: Build relationships with other businesses and organizations that could be critical partners during a recession. Creating and expanding on your channel is critical for success during a recession.

Additional Core Customer Work: Customer retention and loyalty - Develop strategies for retaining customers and keeping them loyal during uncertain economic times.

Part 3 – Create Your Agenda

Now that you understand the components of the agenda, it is time to create your own. Using the suggested agenda as a guide, along with your own research and analysis, carefully consider what elements would best fit your company's specific needs and goals.

Consider incorporating any additional items or areas of focus that you believe would be beneficial to your team. Consider the size and structure of your business, as well as the current state of your finances and operations.

Use the space below to create your agenda.

EXERCISE 7
www.growprofitordie.com

GROW PROFIT OR DIE

List and rank any additional areas within the agenda.

Additional agenda items: price, strategy, decision making, etc.

1 _____

2 _____

3 _____

4 _____

5 _____

6 _____

7 _____

EXERCISE 8

www.growprofitordie.com

GROW PROFIT OR DIE

Create Your Agenda

Primary Objectives In Order	Agenda In Order

Part 4 – Wrap Up

Creating an agenda for a recession-resistant workshop is a crucial step in preparing for a potential economic downturn. By reviewing the suggested agenda and considering the unique needs of your business, you can create a comprehensive and effective plan. It is important to remember that the value of the planning will depend on the preparation and thought put into the agenda. Take the time to consider all aspects of your business, gather the necessary information, and plan for a productive and impactful workshop. With a well-crafted agenda in hand, you and your team will be well equipped to face any economic challenges that may come your way.

Summary of Chapter:

This chapter provides guidelines and recommendations for creating a tailored agenda. The chapter starts with a suggested agenda for a company with $50,000,000-a-year in revenue with about 200 employees, and then explains the importance of each component. It also offers additional agenda items to consider, based on specific business needs. To create a personalized agenda, the chapter encourages readers to review and edit the suggested agenda, considering their company's unique needs and goals. Thorough preparation and planning are necessary to ensure a productive and impactful planning meeting or workshop that equips the team to face potential economic challenges.

Task List for This Chapter:

☐ 1. Review the suggested agenda provided in Chapter 3.

☐ 2. List key outcomes you hope to achieve.

☐ 3. Adjust the suggested agenda to fit your specific business needs (add/remove topics, reorder agenda items, allocate time for discussions).

☐ 4. Review the additional agenda items provided in Part 2 and consider incorporating any relevant topics to your customized agenda.

☐ 5. Create a personalized agenda for your recession-resistant planning using the space provided in Part 3.

☐ 6. Gather relevant data, facts, and information about your business to be used during the in-person meetings.

☐ 7. Designate a trained facilitator to lead specific sections of the workshop (e.g., Recession War Game and Cash Flow).

☐ 8. Ensure all participants are informed about the agenda and expectations regarding their time and desired input.

☐ 9. Plan for regular follow-up meetings or progress reports after the work is done to ensure the plan is on track.

☐ 10. Finalize your agenda and distribute it to all participants ahead of your first meeting or workshop.

Chapter 4 – A "How to" on the Sections of the Agenda

Overview

Based on our suggested agenda, this chapter will review how to facilitate each session on the agenda. Our goal is to give you guidelines and tips on how to run each part of the agenda to help you achieve maximum output from your team. Keep in mind, if you decide NOT to hold a full- day workshop, you can take each of these sections and either do them in separate team setting or another meeting. While we believe the workshop is the best format, feel free to run each of these sections as best suites you.

This chapter is intended to describe how to run each part of the day or each agenda item. Review this prior to starting the day to have a good understanding of how to approach each hour or subject. Also, it is recommended that you have this workbook with you as a guide while running each agenda item. Have the workbook open to help keep you on track, so that you will not miss anything of value.

Be aware of time. As you go over these pages, mark up and track time closely as there is a lot to do, and it will take considerable work to stay on track.

Let's start with some basic facilitation tips. Running a day-long meeting is a skill that needs to be developed, and the tips below may make your day a little easier.

Be aware of time. As you go over these pages, mark up and track time closely as there is a lot to do, and it will take considerable work to stay on track.

Facilitation Tips

Facilitating a one-day workshop with a leadership team of executives can be a challenging task, but with the right preparation and approach, it can be a highly rewarding and productive experience for all involved. Here are some tips for a successful workshop:

Time Management: Manage time effectively and keep the team engaged by prioritizing key discussion points, while also allowing for ample time for exploration and debate. Be mindful of the schedule and watch the clock so that everyone stays on track.

> *Pro Tip – To keep track of time, find the person that best fits these characteristics – perfectionist, meticulous, nitpicky, obsessive or detail-oriented – and make this person the timekeeper.*

EXERCISE 9
www.growprofitordie.com

Recession-Resistant Planning Workshop or Meeting Format

Although we feel that a full-day workshop is the best format, this may not work for your company. If you have decided NOT to do a full-day workshop, what format will you use?

Extra time in regular meetings? Team meetings? Once-a-month meetings?

What topics will you cover for each meeting?

Date	Time	Topic

GROW PROFIT OR DIE

Documentation: Ensure that all ideas and decisions are captured and documented in a format that is easily accessible and reviewable. Consider using digital tools like Miro or OneNote to keep track of the discussions.

Prework: Encourage participants to come prepared with their thoughts and ideas by using electronic forms or other tools to gather information before the workshop. This will help to maximize the time spent during the workshop and help guarantee that everyone is on the same page.

Inclusive Discussions: Ensure that all voices are heard and that everyone has an opportunity to contribute to the discussions. Encourage participation from all members of the team, and actively seek out the opinions of quieter members.

Mix Things Up: Avoid monotony by mixing up the format of the workshop. Consider splitting the team into smaller groups for discussion or using an online tool to gather ideas. Chances are, smaller teams will come to the same conclusion as the larger team, and by splitting up, you can get more tasks done with less time. Taking regular breaks every hour can also help to recharge the team's energy and maintain focus.

> *Pro Tip – To do this work, it is important to have a large room. Take advantage of a large room by having some of the exercises done as smaller groups in different parts of the room. When the assigned time is up, have them report back.*

Assign Roles: Assign specific roles to different members of the team, such as timekeeper or scribe, to keep everyone engaged and invested in the workshop.

Regular Breaks: Regular breaks every hour can help to recharge the team's energy and improve focus. Encourage the team to take a break and stretch their legs, get some fresh air, or grab a snack.

Embracing Technology: Instead of limiting the use of technology, encourage the team to use it to enhance the workshop experience. Provide guidelines for responsible use and ensure that everyone is mindful of the purpose of the workshop and stays focused on the task at hand.

Start and End on Time: This sets the tone for the day and shows respect for everyone's time.

Create a Safe Space: Encourage open and honest communication, and create a nonjudgmental environment where everyone feels comfortable sharing their thoughts and opinions.

> *Pro Tip – Despite the fact that you might not need a safe space, there are almost always members of the team that do. It may feel like the everyone gets a trophy approach. However, it's not, and it's important.*

Encourage Active Listening: Encourage the participants to listen to each other and understand different perspectives. This will lead to more productive and meaningful discussions.

Use Visual Aids: Use visual aids like slides, flip charts, and whiteboards to help convey information, keep the participants engaged, and capture key points and decisions made during the workshop.

Check for Understanding: Throughout the workshop, ask questions and check for understanding to make certain everyone is on the same page.

Have Fun: While the workshop is focused on serious topics, try to incorporate fun activities or games to break the monotony and keep the participants engaged and energized.

Follow-Up: After the workshop, follow up with the participants to guarantee they understand the next steps and to provide any additional support they may need.

Part 1 – Agenda Item - Introduction and Overview of the Day

Begin the workshop with an introduction and overview of the day. Commence the session by starting with a round of good news or highlighting the positive aspects of the company. This will help to set a positive tone for the day and create a better meeting environment. We recommend having a short 5-minute kick-off activity to get the team thinking positively.

It is vital to have a clear purpose and goal for the work you are doing, and this should be introduced by either the facilitator or the leader of the company. A round-the-room feedback session can be conducted to gather the participants' expectations and get their buy-in. It is essential to make sure that the team is aligned on why they are present in the room.

A brief review of the agenda can get everyone on the same page and give them a clear understanding of the objectives for the day. While this may seem redundant, it is essential to make sure that everyone has read the agenda and is aware of the best ways to utilize their time. Keeping the review to a maximum of 5 minutes can help to avoid any unnecessary debates or discussions.

Setting expectations for the day is crucial. Remind the participants why they were selected for the workshop. The facilitator or the CEO should have a list of expectations for the outcome of the day, and this should be shared with the team to ensure that everyone is aligned.

"The CEO should have a list of expectations for the outcome of the day, and this should be shared with the team to ensure that everyone is aligned."

Finally, we recommend leaving a few minutes at the end of the introduction to allow the team to review the prework and pre-reads. This will help to put everyone on the same page and make sure that everyone is aware of the important data.

Call the meeting to order and move to the next session.

Part 2 – Agenda Item - Recession War Game/Simulation

The Recession War Game is an important part of the workshop, but it can also be the most challenging to run. The reason for this is that it is an organic process that is difficult to script. However, let me provide you with a general outline and ideas for conducting this activity.

Before beginning, keep in mind that this is your meeting, so tailor the War Game to your team's needs. Think of it as playing a game of *Monopoly or Risk*, but you will be creating scenarios and rules as you go along, since each business is unique.

The War Game, or Rehearsal, is a crucial simulation of what a potential recession might look like for your company, allowing you to plan and prepare for various scenarios. This workshop is designed to provide a hands-on, experiential learning opportunity, where you can test and refine your strategies in a controlled environment. The key thing to remember is that this is a *SIMULATION*. By simulating the impact of a recession on your business, you can better understand the potential challenges and opportunities and develop a more robust and effective response plan.

As you run the War Game, avoid the temptation to go deep into the P&L statement, because you will get a chance to do that in the afternoon. Part of the simulation will be to create a fictitious P&L that explores the impact of various changes. However, avoid the deep dive on the P&L for this session.

To run this section, it is important to have the company's financials readily accessible. Ideally, you should have more than one screen, with a very large

EXERCISE 9

www.growprofitordie.com

GROW PROFIT OR DIE

List of Expectations for the Outcome of the Recession-Resistant Readiness Workshop

The CEO should have a list of expectations for the outcome of the day, and this should be shared with the team to be sure that everyone is aligned.

1 _____

_____

2 _____

_____

3 _____

_____

4 _____

_____

5 _____

_____

6 _____

_____

7 _____

_____

8 _____

_____

9 _____

_____

main screen to accommodate all the data and ensure everyone can see it. Even if everyone is in the same room, it is best to share one screen across devices so that everyone can follow along.

> *"Avoid the temptation to go deep into the P&L. You will get a chance to do that in the afternoon."*

One person should be designated to run the spreadsheet. This person should be a good communicator and should focus on keeping the spreadsheet simple so that everyone can understand it. Although this person can be the financial person, it is more important to have someone who can communicate well and simplify the information.

> *Pro Tip – Make sure someone builds and tests a spreadsheet for this section prior to the meeting. It will speed things up and reduce wait times.*

Stage One: Begin by creating a simple 6-to-24-month budget, running month to month, for a normal 1-2 year cycle. This should be quick and easy. The purpose is to get everyone on the same page, understanding what a good year looks like without a significant recession headwind.

> *Knowing how aligned the team is can make all the difference as you enter into a recession. Being out of alignment can be one of the most difficult areas for a team to overcome when solving the difficult issues of a recession. Knowing the alignment of the team will make the whole process worth it.*

Stage Two: Once everyone agrees on the running projection of a good year, conduct a brainstorming session. Ask the question, "If a recession were to occur, what would change in these projections?" Capture this information, as it will be valuable later and will lead to great discussion topics. We strongly recommend capturing any list in bullet-point form. Also, bring up any ideas from the prework. Create a copy of the spreadsheet and change the numbers based on what was discussed, calling this the worst-case scenario.

Stage Three: If you have gathered good input, you should now have a great list of what could happen to the business and how it will affect the numbers. In this stage, you can go into as much detail as you like and create a third spreadsheet. Consider what steps you would take to mitigate the headwinds or challenges. For example, if you said in Stage Two that you would lose 35% of your core business in months 3-6, resulting in a $4M deficit, in Stage Three, consider options such as reducing staff, discounting product to sell more, drawing from a line of credit, or borrowing from the owner. Note these changes and adjust the new spreadsheet.

Throughout this process, keep a list of all the changes and their effects. The list can be in Excel, but it should be separate from the spreadsheets, and it should be a running record of both the effects and changes.

Stage Four: After the discussion and the rehearsal of what could happen and what can be done in Stage Two and Three, rank the list of effects and changes. We recommend ranking them in categories such as likelihood of occurrence, level of impact, difficulty to overcome, and long-term effect on the business. You can create your own categories or add more, but this ranking will not determine anything significant at this stage. It will, however, provide great points to discuss later and will be critical to your written plan.

EXERCISE 10
www.growprofitordie.com

GROW PROFIT OR DIE

War Game Simulation/Stage Two

What Could Happen During a Recession?

Based on the War Game, what might happen during a recession?

1 _____

2 _____

3 _____

4 _____

5 _____

6 _____

7 _____

8 _____

9 _____

10 _____

What would happen during a worst-case scenario?

1 _____

2 _____

3 _____

4 _____

5 _____

EXERCISE 11
www.growprofitordie.com

GROW PROFIT OR DIE

Proposed Changes for a Recession

What changes will we make if there is a recession (e.g., reducing staff, discounting products, drawing from a line of credit)? Assign responsibilities for items that you plan to implement.

1 _____

2 _____

3 _____

4 _____

5 _____

6 _____

7 _____

At what point during the recession will changes be made?

How will we handle possible layoffs?

EXERCISE 12
www.growprofitordie.com

GROW PROFIT OR DIE

War Game Stage Three

Proposed Changes	Effects on Business

> Pro Tip – Be ready. You will not have enough time, so be aware of the clock.

Stage Five: Wrap It Up – If time allows, continue the discussion or War Game. At some point, you will either run out of **time** or ideas. It is important to wrap up the session with any final thoughts from the team and make bullet-points of all the findings. Conducting the War Game will generate many ideas and potential challenges that will need to be addressed during a recession, and it is one of the most important reasons to do these activities.

"Conducting the War Game will generate many ideas and potential challenges that will need to be addressed during a recession, and it is one of the most important reasons to do these activities."

Prior to moving to the next session, be sure to take a break and engage the team in something (snack, coffee, stretches) that will increase the energy level and focus of the team prior to moving to the next agenda item.

Additional things to think about as you run the Recession War Game to get the best performance out of your team:

- **Clarify the objective of the Recession War Game:** State the purpose and goals of the war game, so that the team knows what they are trying to achieve and can work together effectively.

- **Emphasize the importance of participation:** Encourage active participation and engagement from all members of the team. This will help everyone to be on the same page and enable all ideas to be considered.

- **Provide clear instructions:** Ensure that the instructions for each stage of the Recession War Game are clear, concise, and easy to follow. This will help keep the process on track and minimize confusion.

- **Encourage creative thinking:** Encourage the team to think creatively and outside the box when considering possible scenarios and solutions. This will help generate a wide range of ideas and potential solutions.

- **Consider the use of additional tools and resources:** Consider incorporating tools and resources that can help facilitate the War Game, such as visual aids, templates, or interactive software. These can help keep the process organized and efficient.

- **Plan for adequate time:** Allow sufficient time for each stage of the Recession War Game, and make sure that there are breaks built into the agenda.

- **Summarize key findings:** At the end of the War Game, summarize the key findings and takeaways, and make sure that everyone is on the same page about what was learned and what the next steps are.

Additional War Game/Rehearsal/Simulation Activities to make it more robust:

- Review the SWOT analysis of the company. Determine the strengths, weaknesses, opportunities, and threats of the company in the event of a recession.

- Determine the company's critical success factors. Identify what factors are most important for the company's success during a recession.

- Establish a scenario-planning process. Create multiple hypothetical scenarios that could occur during a recession and assess the impact on the company's finances.

- Assess the company's resilience. Evaluate the company's ability to withstand the effects of a recession and determine areas for improvement.

- Identify key risk areas. Determine which areas of the company are most vulnerable to the effects of a recession and take steps to mitigate those risks.

- Develop contingency plans. Create plans to address potential issues that could arise during a recession, such as declining sales or reduced cash flow.

- Evaluate the impact of different recession scenarios on the company's finances. Develop an understanding of the potential impact of different recession scenarios on the company's finances and make decisions accordingly.

- Establish a communication plan. Create a plan for communicating important information to stakeholders — such as employees, customers, and suppliers — during a recession.

> *Pro Tip – Of all the activities we would encourage you to perform, we believe the communication plan is the most critical additional area to consider. You do not need to complete this during this section. However, you should return to your communication plan. It will be an important tool during the recession.*

- Evaluate the company's existing financial systems and processes. Identify areas for improvement and make sure that the company's financial systems and processes are strong enough to withstand the effects of a recession.

- Assess the company's cash position. Develop an understanding of the company's liquidity position and make decisions about preserving cash in the event of a recession.

Part 3 – Agenda Item - Assumptions and Core Customer

After taking a break, it's essential to reflect on what you've learned during the War Game and identify any new assumptions that may have surfaced. This is a valuable step to take, as stepping away from the discussion can often allow the subconscious mind to generate additional insights. Allocate 10 to 15 minutes for this exercise.

Moving on to the topic of core customers is crucial. This is the key to surviving and thriving during a recession. Companies that thrive during tough times understand and cultivate close relationships with their core customers. For many teams, identifying their core customers may be a new exercise.

Flash Back: During the 2008 recession, my previous company got laser focused on a core customer and a segment that helped us to maintain our staffing level with no cuts. We got lucky, because we believed in this product and segment. We did not deviate, and that focus propelled us through the recession. When the economy turned around, we had all of our staff ready to take the market share. And we did!

Start by ensuring that the team is in agreement on who their core customer is. This refers to a type of customer, not an individual customer. Core customers are those who love your product or service, buy regularly, don't dispute price, refer others to your business, and pay on time. Defining their attributes — such as their size, type of person or company, and who they typically interact with in your company — is important.

The book *The Inside Advantage*[1] by Robert Bloom is a useful resource for preparing for this discussion and diving deeper into the concept of core customers. If time permits, a pre-read of the summary would help the team be better prepared for this discussion.

Once you have identified your core customer, have a discussion on how you can optimize your product or service for their needs during a recession. It can be tempting to pivot during a downturn, but it's crucial to keep your core customer in mind as you do so. Consider what they will need and how to keep them, as retaining your best customers during a downturn is easier than finding new ones. Capture the team's thoughts and ideas on this topic.

> *Pro Tip –* In this workbook and in our coaching, we talk at length about focus and avoiding the desire to make a pivot. This cannot be overstated or said often enough. When a deep recession hits, you will be close to a panic mode as you see revenue and customers pull back. The natural inclination is to want to look for a pivot. The challenge is that unless you get very lucky with your pivot (and some do), this is the worst time to be investing in what is a very costly and time-consuming task. In most cases pivots have a low chance of success. Knowing that, you will still be tempted, and you will need to be prepared to resist the urge to pivot. Stay the course, and if you had a solid business going into the recession, it will still be a solid business. If it is not a solid business, make that pivot now, prior to any recession.

End this agenda item by creating a plan for serving your core customer during a recession. Consider what changes you would make, what you would keep the same, and how you can attract more core customers. Having a clear plan in place beforehand can help prevent impulsive and ill-considered decisions during a time of panic. Keeping your core customer at the forefront of your mind will help guide your actions during a recession.

If you want to go deeper, here are some additional tasks to help you better understand your core customer.

Here are a few activities that the team can complete to create their core customer profile based on the book *The Inside Advantage*[2] by Robert Bloom.

- **Conduct market research:** Before identifying the core customer, it is important to understand the market landscape. The team can conduct research to gather information about the target market, competitors, and customer needs.

> *Pro Tip – The idea of market research can be daunting for some companies. Remember, as of 2024 AI has made this process so much easier, and much of this research is available by engaging with AI, like ChatGPT.*

- **Define the customer persona:** The team should work together to create a detailed profile of the ideal customer, including demographic information, pain points, and decision-making factors.

- **Analyze customer behavior:** The team can analyze customer behavior data, such as purchase history and engagement levels, to gain insights into what drives customer loyalty. This can be a critical component to understanding your cash flow. Knowing how and when your customer will buy and having some level of prediction capability will help you manage those difficult cash flow months.

- **Identify customer touchpoints:** The team should identify all the ways that customers interact with the company, such as through the website, customer service, and sales interactions. Know where customers look for information and how they interact with your team. Also, understand what type of messages resonate best with your customers and when and where the customer wants to receive these messages. If you know exactly what to say, but the customer is not hearing it, that is wasted energy. First know where to say it and how they want to receive it. Eliminate wasted effort during a recession.

- **Survey customers:** The team can conduct surveys or focus groups to gather feedback from customers about their experiences and what they value most about the company. In the business platform Scaling Up, it stresses this as one of the 10 most important habits great companies get right[3]. Unfortunately, in most of the companies we have worked with, this does not happen or happens very poorly. Start this process now! Begin getting customer feedback prior to needing it.

- **Evaluate customer feedback:** The team should review the feedback from customers and identify common themes and areas for improvement.

- **Conduct customer interviews:** The team can schedule one-on-one interviews with customers to gain deeper insights into their needs and preferences.

- **Evaluate customer service interactions:** The team should review interactions between customers and customer service to identify opportunities to improve the customer experience.

- By following these tasks, the team can create a comprehensive profile of their core customer, which will help them to better understand and serve their customers during a recession or any other challenging time.

"Knowing how and when your customer will buy and having some level of prediction capability will help you manage those difficult cash flow months."

EXERCISE 13
www.growprofitordie.com

GROW PROFIT OR DIE

Optimization of Product or Services for Your Core Customers
Retaining your core customers is easier than finding new ones.

How could you optimize your product or services for your core customers during a recession?

What will your core customer need during a recession that may be different from what your customer needs now? How can you meet those needs?

What will you do to retain your best customers during a recession?

Define the customer persona. Create a detailed profile of the ideal customer, including demographic information, pain points, and decision-making factors.

EXERCISE 14
www.growprofitordie.com

GROW PROFIT OR DIE

How Well Do You Know Your Customers?

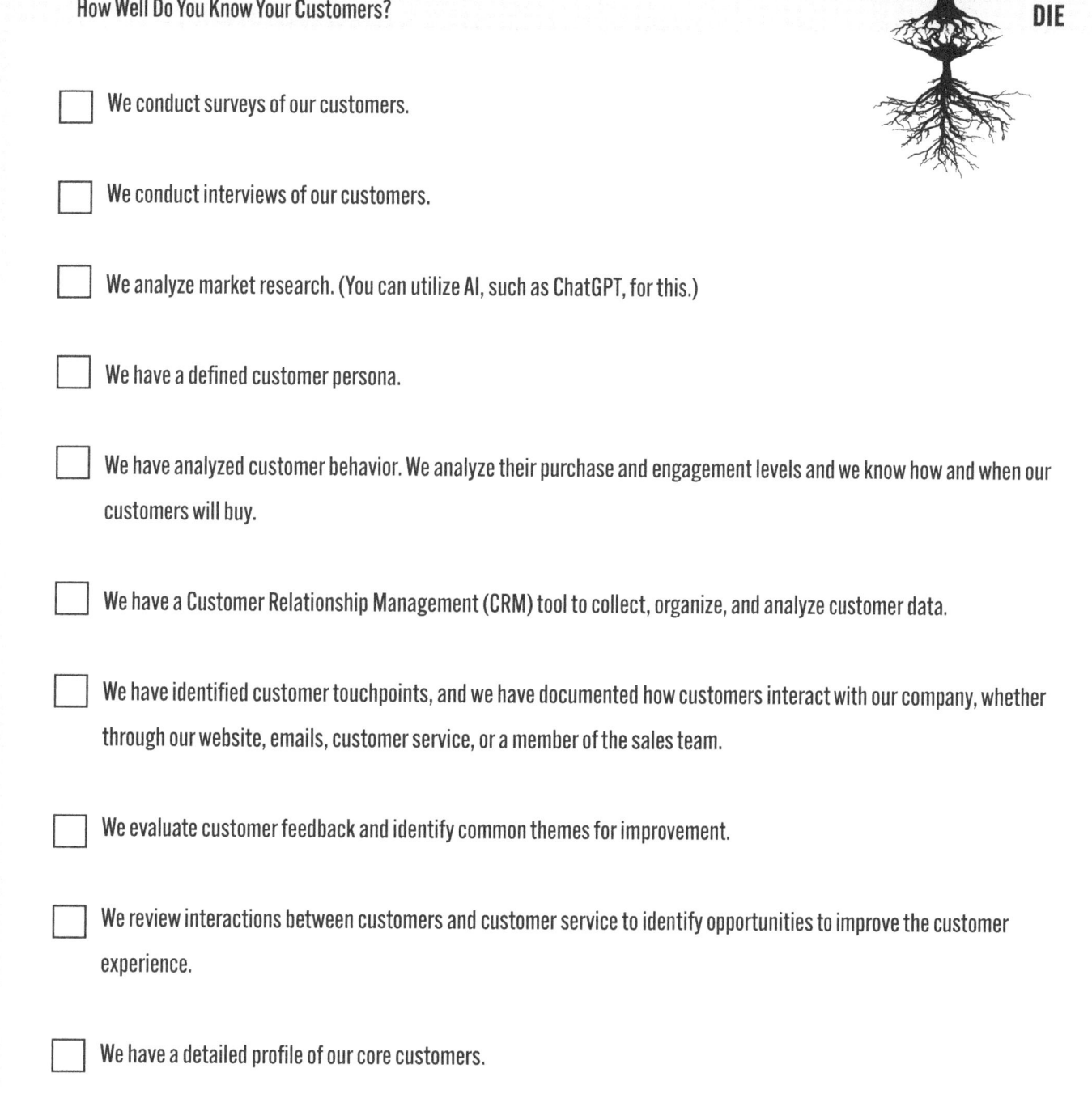

☐ We conduct surveys of our customers.

☐ We conduct interviews of our customers.

☐ We analyze market research. (You can utilize AI, such as ChatGPT, for this.)

☐ We have a defined customer persona.

☐ We have analyzed customer behavior. We analyze their purchase and engagement levels and we know how and when our customers will buy.

☐ We have a Customer Relationship Management (CRM) tool to collect, organize, and analyze customer data.

☐ We have identified customer touchpoints, and we have documented how customers interact with our company, whether through our website, emails, customer service, or a member of the sales team.

☐ We evaluate customer feedback and identify common themes for improvement.

☐ We review interactions between customers and customer service to identify opportunities to improve the customer experience.

☐ We have a detailed profile of our core customers.

Part 4 – Agenda Item - Lunch

Lunchtime is an important opportunity to recharge and refocus for the remainder of the workshop. Whether you have fallen behind schedule or not, taking a break is essential. Even if it's just a short 15-minute break, it is important to step away from work and allow your mind and body to recharge. This break can increase productivity and creativity, making the rest of the workshop more effective.

Additional lunchtime things to consider.

- Encourage socializing and networking among participants. This can foster stronger relationships and collaboration within the team.

- Provide a variety of healthy food options to cater to different dietary needs and preferences.

- Set up a comfortable and relaxing space for attendees to enjoy their lunch, such as a lounge area with soft seating and natural lighting.

-
-

By incorporating these elements, the lunch break can be transformed into a productive and enjoyable time that contributes to the overall success of the workshop.

> *"Even if it's just a short 15-minute break, it is important to step away from work and allow your mind and body to recharge."*

Part 5 – Agenda Item - Staff Assessment

During a recession, many businesses place a strong emphasis on staff and staff retention. This is because staffing costs are often the largest line item in their P&L statement. When the economy changes, staff is usually impacted, and they know it. It is therefore crucial to discuss this issue and to get it right.

Just discussing the company's plans in advance of an economic downturn will have a significant impact on how well you handle the inevitable discussions and decisions during the recession. As the facilitator, it is important to frame this discussion and to ensure that it is viewed from multiple dimensions. Also make certain that everyone on the team has an opportunity to provide input, and that in the end, there is agreement on the plan for addressing any staffing issues.

Stage One: The first step in opening up this dialogue is to verify that everyone has a clear understanding of the staffing costs and requirements. Often, the leadership team does not fully understand the complexities and costs of the current staff, and in nearly every company we review, they are overstaffed for current demand. To avoid this, take 10 to 15 minutes to discuss the costs and requirements.

Stage Two: The next step is to discuss the company's philosophical approach to staffing. For example, if there is a 20% downturn in revenue, but the company is breaking even, do they implement layoffs to return to profitability, or do they run for a few months before doing so? Another example might be what will the company do if there is a 40% downturn in revenue, and the company is incurring negative EBITDA every month, requiring borrowing to keep the business going? How long will they do this, if at all? There are many questions that can be asked and debated by the team. Before concluding this philosophical discussion, it is critical to determine the following: 1) Will staffing costs be cut? 2) How will cuts be made? 3) What order would cuts occur? 4) Will layoffs be the first step, or will salary and benefit cuts be implemented first? 5) Will cuts be made all at once, or gradually over time? This discussion must be robust, and it is crucial to have it now, rather than when you are under the pressure of a recession.

Stage Three: Create a Plan. Based on the discussion, it is critical that the team creates a plan. This could be a simple bullet-point list of values and steps to be taken, as the future is uncertain. It is important that this plan is clear, and that the team agrees to support the final decisions, even if they don't necessarily agree with them. Be aware that if there is a single owner or a partnership of two to three owners, they may dictate the plan, which is acceptable to some extent.

Stage Four: During Stages One, Two, and Three, it may become apparent that some or many of these changes can be made now. This is particularly true if the discussion centers on the number of staff needed to run the business or on underperforming individuals. Whatever is discovered, it is important to decide what changes should be made NOW to run a better business. These changes can be labeled as "Immediate Changes to Prepare for a Recession" or simply "Running Your Business Better." It is important to remind everyone of the natural human tendency toward ease and comfort, and that you should lean more toward tightening your belts before it becomes necessary.

Stage Five: If time permits, it is a good idea to end on a positive note with a brainstorming exercise on what alternatives or possibilities there might be. This is not a commitment to anything, but simply a way to capture brainstorming in the moment when everyone is considering possibilities.

Summary of Tasks:

- Assess the cost of staffing and understand the staffing needs of the company.

- Discuss the philosophical approach to staffing in the event of a downturn in revenue.

- Consider the various options for cutting staff costs, such as layoffs, salary and benefit cuts, or gradual cuts.

- Create a clear plan for addressing staffing issues in the event of a recession.

- Look for opportunities to make changes in the business now to improve efficiency and profitability.

- Engage in a positive brainstorming exercise to consider alternative possibilities and opportunities.

EXERCISE 15

www.growprofitordie.com

Staff Assessment

- [ ] What are your current staffing costs and requirements?

- [ ] What is the company's philosophical approach to staffing?

- [ ] Will staffing costs be cut?

- [ ] How will cuts be made?

- [ ] What order would cuts be made?

- [ ] Will layoffs be the first step, or will salary and benefit cuts be implemented first?

- [ ] Will cuts be made all at once or implemented over time?

- [ ] Are employee evaluations thorough so that the appropriate people can be identified in case a layoff is necessary?

- [ ] Are key performance indicators (KPIs) for people and departments being monitored? If not, what will you do to make those changes? If the economy tightens, you want to be sure to keep your best people, but how will you do that without evaluations and KPIs?

- [ ] What is your plan for staffing during a recession?

GROW PROFIT OR DIE

Part 6 – Agenda Item - P&L Statement

During the first part of the agenda, you will have a high-level overview of the P&L statement and run through various scenarios as part of the War Game/Simulation. The notes and insights from this session will provide valuable input for the deep dive into the P&L that we will conduct in this chapter. The goal is to have you thoroughly examine the P&L and discuss potential actions long before a recession hits, avoiding a panicked approach.

Emphasize: The P&L statement is a crucial aspect of any business and is usually reviewed quarterly or more frequently. While it may be familiar territory for most organizations, it's important to approach it with a fresh perspective and challenge the team to think differently.

Stage One: Review and identify areas for discussion. Provide access to a detailed version of the P&L statement and spend a few minutes diving into its components. Discuss which areas should receive the most focus, avoiding small, insignificant areas like office supplies.

Stage Two: Encourage the team to identify "sacred cows" that no one wants to touch. Simply identifying these areas has significant value, as they may be key during a recession. For example, a sales team's car allowance may be considered a sacred expense but could be adjusted to a mileage reimbursement during a downturn. List these sacred cows and have an open discussion about them. You will be returning to this list someday, so make sure you capture it, not just *talk* about it. True strength is doing the exercises that make us uncomfortable.

> *"Teams that engage in productive conflict know that the only purpose is to produce the best possible solution in the shortest period of time. They discuss and resolve issues more quickly and completely than others, and they emerge from heated debates with no residual feelings or collateral damage, but with an eagerness and readiness to take on the next important issues."* – Patrick Lencioni

Stage Three: Based on the previous discussions, move the team towards creating a plan for improving or changing the P&L statement during a recession. This should be a combination of discussion, collaboration, and debate, with ideas captured and ranked. Some changes may become apparent that do not need to wait for a recession to be implemented. Make a note of these and, if time permits, make a final decision on them. Be sure to have concise notes and bullet points of agreed-upon changes and action items for future reference.

Stage Four: Utilize the remaining time for brainstorming and discussion of alternative revenue sources. Keep the focus on coming up with a list of alternatives and use the lens of what your core customer would want in a potential pivot or diversification. This will increase the likelihood of success. Reference the work from earlier in the day to help guide this discussion.

Note: It's much better to start diversifying or pivoting your revenue before any troubles arise, rather than waiting for a crisis. Many businesses panic and try to diversify at the worst possible time. If you have a good idea, don't wait for a recession to experiment. We have reminded you of this multiple times in this workbook because it is so important.

EXERCISE 16

www.growprofitordie.com

Profit & Loss Statement

Thoroughly examine the P&L statement and discuss potential actions long before a recession hits. Ask these questions to become more recession resistant.

- [ ] Which areas should receive the most focus?

- [ ] Which areas are insignificant and will result in only minor savings?

- [ ] What are the sacred cows that no one wants to touch? For example, is the sales team's car allowance a sacred cow?

- [ ] What changes can be made that will have a big impact on the P&L statement?

- [ ] What are alternative revenue sources? (Look at this through the lens of the core customer. What type of pivot or diversification would a core customer want?)

- [ ] What can you do to improve cash flow? Can you increase prices or ask for 15-day terms instead of 30?

- [ ] How will you manage debt during a recession? Do you have access to loans or a credit line?

GROW PROFIT OR DIE

> *"First, you fire bullets (low-cost, low-risk, low-distraction experiments) to figure out what will work — calibrating your line of sight by taking small shots. Then, once you have empirical validation, you fire a cannonball (concentrating resources into a big bet) on the calibrated line of sight."*[5] *- Jim Collins*

Part 7 – Agenda Item - Cash Flow

Cash flow is often the first area where the challenges of a recession will show up. It is the key performance indicator that will indicate if there is a problem. However, many small-to-medium-sized businesses do not have adequate ways of tracking or measuring cash flow. As a result, it is crucial to get a handle on measuring and reporting on cash flow before the workshop, if possible.

In a growing company, cash flow is always a challenge, especially during a recession. Some of the discussion should focus on balancing the growth of the company, which strains cash flow, with being adequately prepared for a downturn. This is a difficult issue to consider, but it is important to address it. Take this time to dig in a little. How fast should you grow when you consider cash flow and borrowing? A mature strategy would have this built in, but too often companies can grow without every really weighing this question.

Additional thinking - In the early 90s, Dell faced serious cash flow challenges that threatened the company's growth. But instead of buckling under pressure, they innovated their supply chain, pioneering the direct-to-consumer model.[6] This minimized inventory costs, significantly improved cash flow, and provided a platform for exponential growth. In Dell's case, necessity wasn't just the mother of invention, it was the catalyst for a business model that would revolutionize the industry.

Going into this section, the team may be worn out, but it is essential to make the most of the discussion. Cash flow can be a complex and abstract topic, so it is important to give the team space and get as much accomplished as possible. The topic of cash flow will be revisited multiple times during the recession. If you sense the team does not have the energy for this meaty of a topic, we would recommend scheduling a separate morning meeting later in the week or the next week to discuss this exercise.

Stage One: Utilize "The Power of One" tool from the Scaling Up family of tools and the book *Scaling Up*.[7] This tool reviews the 7 areas within your business that can be improved to increase cash flow. The team should go through this exercise and challenge their assumptions about what can be done in the business. The areas reviewed include volume, price, costs, receivables, payables, and inventory. Capture the ideas and end with a bullet-point list of what can be done.

Stage Two: Open up the discussion and brainstorm additional ways to manage cash flow. Take the list from Stage One and see what the team can add. This is also a good time to debate what would actually be done, such as increasing prices or asking for 15-day terms instead of 30. Rank the ideas and determine what the team would support and implement. Use the Dell example as inspiration or a jumping off point to think about how you would revolutionize your industry.

Stage Three: Create a plan. The team should have a ranked list and be ready to decide on the actions they will take. Encourage the team to implement changes immediately, as many changes made during a recession can also work today.

Stage Four: Discuss debt management, risk management, and decision matrices. During a recession, most companies will lose money at some point during a given month or quarter. It is important to make difficult decisions on when it is smart to go into the red for a short time and when to begin cuts. This decision is often based on the amount of extra cash on hand and access to debt.

During a recession, access to funds can become limited, and banks may enforce covenants that were previously lax. This topic requires a candid and robust discussion. How much of a cash reserve is the company willing to risk? How much of a loan or a credit line will the company consider? How long is the company willing to operate in the red, and under what criteria will it operate in the red? Who makes these decisions is also an important consideration. If necessary, set another meeting to discuss this topic in more detail, as it will impact many of the decisions made during the workshop.

> *Pro Tip* – *During a recession, banks tend to be one of the most panicked institutions. This may seem ironic, as the business leaders with the most money are the ones who are the most alarmed. However, it is important to keep this in mind when planning, as your banking relationship will play a critical role. During the 2008 recession, banks were being bailed out while also ending their relationships with problematic clients or sectors, revoking their lines of credit. Read that again, even if you are doing great, but you are in a problematic sector, the bank could do this to you. This may seem difficult to believe, but it did happen 15 years ago and also in 2001. To prepare for the upcoming recession, it is crucial to plan and strengthen your banking relationship. Contact Red Wagon for tips on this crucial aspect of your business.*

Stage Five: If there is time, brainstorm additional nontraditional cash flow options. It is better to be prepared than to scramble. Think about alternative options, such as a rich uncle, and work from there.

Part 8 – Agenda Item - War Room and the Plan

The War Room and Plan section is a crucial part of preparing for a potential recession. It involves establishing a physical and virtual space for collaboration and data collection, as well as clear communication during the downturn. Also, this section will cover the importance of having leading KPIs and well-defined roles for team members. Finally, to guarantee success, assign people who will be responsible and held accountable for creating and executing the plan.

War Room: To effectively tackle complex issues during a recession, it is important to establish both a physical and virtual War Room. The physical space should be dedicated to idea generation and allow for easy access to data and team collaboration. It also creates a mental shift when you enter that room. In a normal day you will have to keep the business running, or as we say work **in** the business. During a recession, you will have to jump from working **in** the business to working **on** the business on a fairly frequent basis. The frequency will be more than during a normal business cycle. There is a reason governments have specific rooms dedicated to war-time activity. In the normal course of any government, they run the affairs of the country, but at times, they have to jump into *war time* mode. It is no different for you working in and on the business. During a recession, we believe it is important to have a physical place to do this.

The virtual War Room should utilize modern collaboration tools, such as Teams or Miro, to work on issues remotely. Similar to the above physical War Room, you will want a virtual space as well.

War Room Communication: Clear and regular communication is crucial during a recession. Discussing communication strategies in advance can help make certain that the team stays informed and on the same page during a crisis.

Your team will be looking to the leadership of the company to keep them in the loop more than during your typical quarter. Your team will want to go the extra mile on communication, potentially using additional tools, and being sure to inform people about critical pieces of information. During COVID-19, many companies did weekly update videos. These small videos were a significant help in aiding communication.

> *Pro Tip –* *Well-made videos from the CEO or leadership will be critical during this time. The good news is a well-made video is not difficult to do. It requires solid audio and lightening and a small amount of editing. All these things can be done internally and should be done. If you are not in the habit of using video to communicate with your organization, we recommend getting started. Also, transcripts can be easily pulled from the video and published for staff that prefer to read the update.*

KPIs: Leading indicators are essential in detecting potential issues early on. It is critical to focus on developing KPIs beyond just cash flow, as lagging indicators, such as revenue by quarter, can cause additional loss if not addressed. Assign a team member with strong accountability and leadership to this task to assess the development and monitoring of KPIs.

Earlier in the book, we talked about the power of associations within your industry that could help you find and track important data. This is also a good time to engage with them.

Roles: Defining and clarifying roles during a stressful and revenue-challenged time is essential. Consider how roles may shift, such as sales or finance taking on a leadership role, and how HR or IT may need to adapt. Having a clear understanding of roles and scope of power before a crisis can provide better direction and clarity during a downturn.

Prior to a recession, the different roles in a company are often not adequately defined. In addition, companies do not always make it clear who is accountable for making sure that a task is completed. If that is the case with your company, this is the perfect time to clear that up for normal operating times. Once you have that, provide written guidelines for how roles and accountability may shift during a recession.

Accountability for the Plan: As the facilitator, it is important to assign tasks and hold team members accountable for creating and executing the plan that will be produced. Decide who will build the plan, track proposed changes, and hold people accountable. Consider whether the plan will be reported on regularly at meetings or if it will wait until there are more indicators of a recession. Discuss and decide on these details in advance to secure the success of the plan.

Part 9 - Agenda Item Wrap-Up and Additional Items: End the day on a positive note. Make sure to thank the team, highlight the wins and close strong. Have emails or cascading communication for the day ready to go, so that you can keep the ball rolling right at the end.

Capture Major Decisions from the Day: During the day, you will make some major decisions about how you will run your business on a day-to-day basis, not just during a recession. It is critical to capture those major decisions and document who is accountable for them. For example, you might have decided that sales and marketing need to be combined now and that the sales manager will be accountable for both, with the marketing manager reporting up. Ok... Is that captured? Who is accountable to do it? When are the deadlines? How will the team communicate?

When you make it through an agenda this intense, you are bound to make some important decisions. Just make sure you capture them and follow up!

Congratulations on a successful workshop!

Summary of Chapter:

This chapter outlines guidelines and tips for facilitating each part of the recommended agenda to help maximize team output. It offers facilitation tips for a successful meeting, emphasizing the importance of time management, documentation, prework, inclusive discussions, using technology, and more. The chapter covers how to handle each part of the agenda, including setting a positive tone, running a Recession War Game simulation, addressing staffing issues, and conducting deep dives into the P&L statement and cash flow. It also emphasizes the importance of having a War Room and a well-defined plan in place to prepare for a potential recession, assigning clear roles and responsibilities, and planning for accountability.

EXERCISE 17

www.growprofitordie.com

Who Will Take Responsibility for Implementing Changes?

When conducting the workshop, you will discover changes in your business that you can make today to help make it more profitable. Assign one person to be accountable for each action.

GROW PROFIT OR DIE

Primary Objectives In Order	Who is responsible? If more than one person works on this project, who is responsible for overseeing it?	Due Date	Action Completed (Yes/No/Partially Completed)

(Many people may be required to complete one action step, but one person needs to be in charge of making sure the action item is completed.)

Task List for This Chapter:

- [ ] 1. Review facilitation tips for conducting a successful meeting.

- [ ] 2. Prepare an introduction and overview of the day.

- [ ] 3. Plan the execution of the Recession War Game/Simulation.

- [ ] 4. Reflect on the War Game results and identify new assumptions.

- [ ] 5. Discuss and define core customer attributes.

- [ ] 6. Plan and facilitate a productive lunch break.

- [ ] 7. Conduct a staff assessment to address staffing issues.

- [ ] 8. Thoroughly examine the P&L statement and identify potential actions.

- [ ] 9. Assess cash flow management and tracking methods.

- [ ] 10. Establish a War Room and plan, including KPIs and defined roles.

- [ ] 11. Assign accountability for creating and executing the plan.

- [ ] 12. Prepare a wrap-up communication to end the workshop on a positive note.

Chapter 5 – Conclusion

As we reach the conclusion of this book, let's reflect on the journey we have embarked upon. We discussed the importance of preparing for a recession and how to organize a successful workshop. In addition, we also listed relevant data that should be gathered, and we provided guidance to help you develop a comprehensive agenda. We have covered a wealth of information that will empower you and your team to face potential economic challenges head-on.

The key takeaways from this workbook are the importance of proactive preparation, effective decision-making, and fostering a resilient business operation. By investing the time and resources into conducting a recession-preparation workshop prior to a recession, you are not only setting your business up for success during a downturn, but you are also enhancing its overall competitiveness and long-term health.

As you move forward, remember that the insights and strategies outlined in this book are meant to serve as a foundation upon which you can build and customize your approach. The real value of the workshop lies in the active engagement of your team, the honest evaluation of your current business practices, and the identification and implementation of necessary changes.

To verify that the insights gained from the process are internalized and translated into action, we recommend incorporating feedback and reflection prompts throughout the process. Encourage participants to share their thoughts, concerns, and suggestions, both during and after the bulk of the work is done. This will help foster a culture of continuous learning and improvement, ultimately enabling your business to navigate any economic challenge that may arise.

We would like to acknowledge the countless contributors, experts, and sources that have helped shape this workbook. Their knowledge, experience, and guidance have been invaluable in creating a comprehensive and practical resource. We encourage you to explore the resources and tools mentioned throughout the book to further enhance your understanding and preparation.

With the tools and knowledge gained from this workbook, you are now better equipped to grow your profit and strengthen your business in the face of any recession. We wish you the best of luck on this journey and look forward to hearing about your successes and the key concepts you have learned and implemented. Remember, the time to prepare is now. Embrace the challenge, and let the growth begin.

As we send you off, we have covered various aspects of recession-resistant preparation and how to conduct a workshop to make certain your business thrives during economic challenges. Now, let's summarize the key action items that will enable you to implement the insights and strategies discussed throughout the book:

1. **Plan your workshop:** Set a date, identify the right participants, and allocate the necessary resources. This will provide the basis for a successful event.

2. **Develop a custom agenda:** Utilize the guidance provided in Chapter 3 to create an agenda tailored to your business needs, outlining topics, activities, and timelines.

3. **Gather essential data:** Follow the recommendations in Chapter 2 to collect crucial data and information that will inform your decision-making.

4. **Engage your team:** Encourage active participation, open communication, and collaboration among all participants.

5. **Review and refine business practices:** Critically assess your current operations and identify areas for improvement or potential pivots that could lead to increased revenue or profit.

6. **Implement necessary changes:** Develop a plan for implementing the insights and strategies identified and assign responsibilities to verify follow-through.

7. **Foster a culture of continuous learning:** Incorporate feedback and reflection prompts to encourage ongoing learning and improvement within your organization.

8. **Monitor progress and adjust as needed:** Regularly evaluate the effectiveness of the changes implemented and adjust as required to safeguard continued success and resilience.

9. **Stay informed:** Keep abreast of economic trends and forecasts to anticipate potential challenges and adapt your strategies accordingly.

10. **Share your insights and successes:** Share your experiences and insights with other businesses, fostering a supportive community that can collectively overcome economic challenges.

By following these action items and proactively preparing for a potential recession, you are positioning your business for success and growth, regardless of the economic climate. Remember, the key to navigating economic challenges is proactive preparation, informed decision-making, and a resilient and adaptable business operation.

As we close this book, I can't help but look back. I remember my journey through the 2008-2009 recession. The challenges we overcame as a team made us stronger, and our success in the years following the recession were directly related to that adversity. We had prepared for parts of the recession before it hit, so we just executed a plan when the time came. Please learn from my experience, and create a plan for your upcoming recession.

About the Author

As a successful entrepreneur with over 20 years of experience, Wade Wyant has a wealth of knowledge and expertise to share. Throughout his career, Wade has started several businesses and achieved remarkable success. His last company, which he successfully built and grew during the 2008 recession, was sold in 2017. Over the course of 15 years running this business, Wade led his company to six appearances on the Inc. 5000 list, several Entrepreneur of the Year awards, and helped hundreds of Fortune 500 clients secure their digital systems. With an impressive annual revenue of over $40 million and a team of over 100 employees, Wade has proven his ability to build and lead a successful business.

In addition to his business acumen, Wade has valuable experience navigating the challenges of a recession. Despite facing moments of doubt during the 2008 financial crisis, his company not only survived, but thrived. By carefully planning and maintaining strong values, Wade's company doubled its growth every two years for the next six years. In the years following the recession, Wade used the lessons he learned to help other companies through his advisory business, Red Wagon Advisors.

Now, Wade is sharing his knowledge and experience with business owners and executives who may not have had the opportunity to lead their companies through a recession. With his extensive background and proven track record, Wade is well equipped to help others navigate these challenges and come out on the other side stronger and more successful. Whether you're a seasoned entrepreneur or just starting out, this workbook will provide valuable insights and practical guidance that you can use to prepare your business for the next recession.

Connect with Wade on Minnect

Glossary of Key Terms

A

AI – Artificial intelligence, which can be used for various tasks, including writing documents with input from someone, analyzing trends, and searching for relevant data

B

Balance sheet – a summary of a business's financial information, including assets, liabilities, and shareholder's equity

C

Cash flow statement – statement that includes all the cash that flows into a company during a certain period of time

ChatGPT – AI, or artificial intelligence, that assists people with writing

Customer data – Information about customers, which includes customer preferences, buying habits, and behavior; customer data is crucial for market analysis and can be gathered through customer surveys, market research, and data analytics

Competitor analysis – An analysis of the competition, which includes their strengths, weaknesses, and strategies; gather this information through examining the competition's websites, financial statements and by conducting market research

Core customers – refers to a type of customer who loves your product or service, buys regularly, doesn't dispute price, refers others to your business and pays on time; determine the attributes of your core customers by defining what type of person or company typically loves your product or service

CRM system – a Customer Relationship Management (CRM) system can help businesses collect, organize, and analyze customer data

Customer persona – a detailed profile of the ideal customer, including demographic information, pain points, and decision-making factors

Customer segmentation – the practice of segmenting your customers into groups based on similar characteristics, such as buying habits, age, preferences

Customer touchpoints – the way customers interact with your business, including your website, sales representatives, and customer service

E

EBITDA – Earnings before interest, taxes, depreciation and amortization

Economic indicators – economic indicators include such things as inflation, unemployment rates, and Gross Domestic Product (GDP); these indicators provide insight into the overall health of the economy and help businesses make informed decisions

F

Free cash flow – the money remaining after operating expenses and capital expenditures have been paid

G

Gross Domestic Product – the market value of all the goods and services for a country for an entire year

I

Income statement – a statement that includes a company's income and expenses, including whether or not the company is making a profit

Industry trends and reports – This includes reports from industry associations, research firms, and government agencies. These reports provide a comprehensive overview of the industry, including growth rates, market size, and trends.

J

Just-in-time manufacturing model – a model that focuses on providing inventory just in time to meet the demands of customers, without storing excess inventory; this model increases profitability

K

KPIs- key performance indicators; KPIs may vary by industry; for recession-resistant planning, KPIs include completing projects within their timelines, adherence to budget and resource constraints, quality and effectiveness of proceedings; number of participants and their level of engagement, success and impact of implementing the action plan

M

Market analysis – an analysis of the current and future trends of the market to help businesses understand their competition, customer preferences, market opportunities, and potential risks; to analyze your market, gather the following information: industry trends and reports, customer data, competitor analysis, market demographics, economic indicators, sales and revenue data

Market demographics – demographic information such as age, gender, income, and education level; market demographics help businesses target their audience and make informed decisions

Microsoft Forms –an online tool for creating polls, surveys, and quizzes

Miro – a virtual whiteboard with extensive tools for collaboration

N

Net cash flow – the difference between cash outflow and inflow, and this amount can be positive or negative depending on whether or not a company made a profit

O

One Note – a digital note-taking application that allows participants to collaborate and capture text, audio, images, and video

One-page strategic plan – a concise business plan developed by Scaling Up

Operating cash flow – the amount of cash a company earns within a certain time period

Pivot – a change that affects the business operations, especially products and services

Profit and loss statement (P&L) – this statement should include revenue, cost of goods sold, gross profit, operating expenses, and net income; use graphs, charts, and tables when presenting your P&L statement

Power of One – tool from Scaling Up that helps businesses improve cash flow; tool included in Scaling Up by Verne Harnish

R

Recession – a widespread decline in the economy that lasts more than a few months

Recession War Game – a simulation of a planning session that would occur if a company were actually experiencing a recession

S

Safe space – a place where open and honest communication can occur

Staffing analysis – staffing information that includes employee headcount, department staffing levels, employee performance data, third-party payroll data

Supply chain analysis – a careful analysis of suppliers to ensure that your company has a reliable supply of inventory

SWOT analysis – companies analyze their strengths, weaknesses, opportunities, and threats.

W

War room – a separate space to tackle the tough issues that arise during a recession

Resources

AI

- ChatGPT

Books

- *Hyper Sales Growth: Street-Proven Systems & Processes* by Jack Daly
- *Scaling Up: How a Few Companies Make It … and Why the Rest Don't* by Verne Harnish
- *Traction: Get a Grip on Your Business* by Gino Wickman
- *Wake-Up Call: Insights for Entrepreneurs to Have More Freedom, Reduce Drama, and Scale Their Businesses* by Wade Wyant
- *The Five Dysfunctions of a Team: A Workshop for Team Leaders* by Patrick Lencioni
- *The inside Advantage: The Strategy That Unlocks the Hidden Growth in Your Business* by Robert H. Bloom and Dave Conti

Data Analytic Tools

- Google Analytics
- SEMRush
- Moz

Online Tools

- Microsoft Forms –an online tool for creating polls, surveys, and quizzes
- Microsoft Teams – a communication platform that allows businesses to collaborate; features differ between versions

www.growprofitordie.com

- Miro – a virtual whiteboard with extensive tools for collaboration
- One Note – a digital note-taking application that allows participants to collaborate and capture text, audio, images, and video

Physical Tools

- Notebooks and pens – People may enjoy personal notebooks to jot their thoughts and keep with them
- Post-it notes – These small notes are great for brainstorming, voting, or prioritizing ideas
- Timer – This tool can help keep the workshop on schedule
- Whiteboard and markers – For a face-to-face meeting, whiteboards can provide an interactive means of capturing the ideas of the team

Here are a few of the books and authors that influenced my thinking:

Scaling Utp: How a Few Companies Make It . . . and Why the Rest Don't by Verne Harnish

Good to Great: Why Some Companies Make the Leap . . . And Other's Don't by Jim Collins

Disney War by James B. Stewart

Let's Get Real or Let's Not Play: Transforming the Buyer/Seller Relationship by Mahan Khalsa

The 4 Disciplines of Execution: Achieving Your Wildly Important Goals by Chris McChesney

Shoe Dog: A Memoir by the Creator of Nike by Phil Knight

Topgrading: The Proven Hiring and Promoting Method That Turbocharges Company Performance by Bradford D. Smart

Multipliers: How the Best Leaders Make Everyone Smarter by Liz Wiseman

Predictable Revenue: Turn Your Business into a Sales Machine with the $100 Million Best Practices of Salesforce.com by Aaron Ross and Marylou Tyler

Blue Ocean Strategy: How to Create Uncontested Market Space and Make the Competition Irrelevant by W. Chan Kim and Renee A. Mauborgne

Trillion Dollar Coach: The Leadership Playbook of Silicon Valley's Bill Campbell by Eric Schmidt, Jonathan Rosenberg, and Alan Eagle

Humanocracy: Creating Organizations as Amazing as the People Inside Them by Gary Hamel and Michele Zanini

Turning the Flywheel: A Monograph to Accompany Good to Great by Jim Collins

What Got You Here Won't Get You There: How Successful People Become Even More Successful by Marshall Goldsmith

Nine Lies About Work: A Freethinking Leader's Guide to the Real World by Marcus Buckingham and Ashley Goodall

The Infinite Game by Simon Sinek

The Vision Driven Leader: 10 Questions to Focus Your Efforts, Energize Your Team, and Scale Your Business by Michael Hyatt

Profit First: Transform Your Business from a Cash-Eating Monster to a Money-Making Machine by Mike Michalowicz

Hyper Sales Growth: Street-Proven Systems & Processes. How to Grow Quickly & Profitably by Jack Daly

The Future Is Faster Than You Think: How Converging Technologies Are Transforming Business, Industries, and Our Lives by Peter H. Diamandis and Steven Kotler

Antifragile: Things That Gain from Disorder by Nassim Nicholas Taleb

Be 2.0 (Beyond Entrepreneurship 2.0) by Jim Collins

Additional Resources

Thanks for being dedicated to becoming Recession Resistant.

We've got some extra resources for you:

- Recession-Resistant Starter Guide
- Recession-Resistant Infograph
- *Wake-Up Call* Chapters
- Upcoming Books
- Recession-Resistant Workshops
- Glossary of Key Terms

Keep up the good work!

www.growprofitordie.com

ADVANCED READERS COPY Uncorrected Proof | Wade W. Wyant

RECESSION RESISTANT
STARTER GUIDE
Prepare for the Unexpected

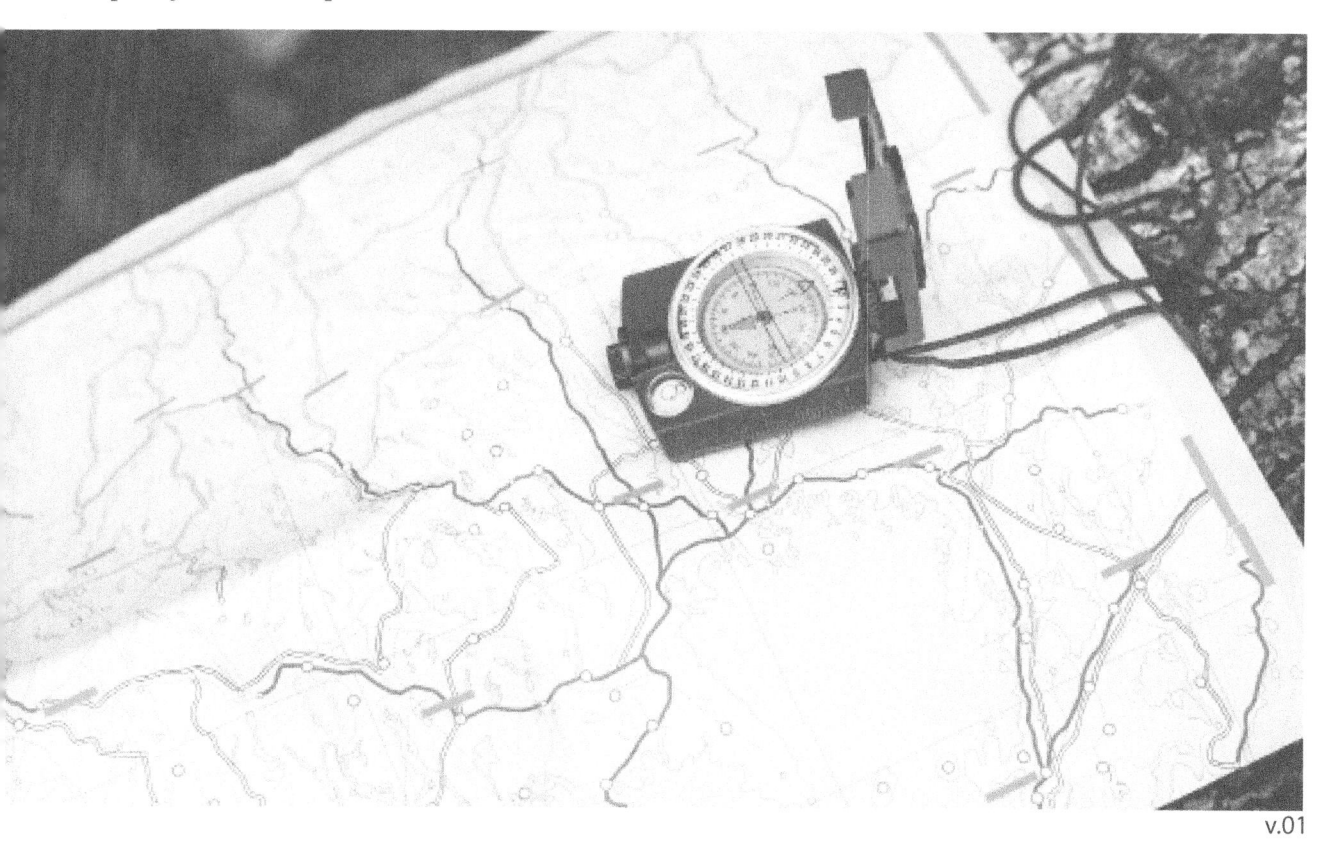

v.01

Recession Resistant
Prepare For The Unexpected

RED wagon

www.growprofitordie.com

Make Your Business Resistant

Congratulations on taking proactive steps to prepare your business for potential economic challenges. This document provides a rough outline for conducting a one-day recession workshop, designed to equip you with the tools and knowledge necessary to become recession-resistant. At Red Wagon Advisors, we have additional resources available to assist you in your preparation. Whether you opt to facilitate the workshop yourself or bring in a professional from Red Wagon, our goal is to empower you with the comprehensive structure needed to analyze and improve your business. Participating in this workshop will help you identify areas for growth, even in the absence of a recession, and develop a solid plan for success. Don't miss this opportunity to secure your business's future. You can implement this yourself or you can also register for this valuable workshop today.

— WADE.

P.S. It's understandable to feel overwhelmed by the amount of information and data that may be needed for this workshop, but it's important to remember that the objective is to be proactive and prepare for a potential recession. Don't let the pursuit of perfection hold you back from taking the necessary steps. The goal of this workshop is to gather information, assess your current state, and develop a plan. Even if you don't have all the data or information at hand, the process of preparing and participating in the workshop will provide valuable insights and help you better understand the areas that need improvement. The most important thing is to take action and make the most of the time available, as preparation is key to weathering any economic storm.

What You Need to get Started

#1 It is critical to get the date and location set. Do that now, and lock it in. This is too easy to put off. "The fear of doing this will keep you from doing this." -Wade Wyant

    Date:
    Location:

#2 You will need to think carefully on the number of people and who you invite.

- CEO
- CFO
- HR Personnel
- Sales Personnel
- Financial Analyst
- Operational Lead
- Discretionary Staff

Things You Need to Arrange *Before* Meeting

To ensure the best outcome from this workshop, all participants should come prepared with relevant facts and data about their business. This will allow for a more in-depth and personalized approach to each company's unique needs. Before attending, we recommend taking time to think about what could potentially affect your business during a recession, including market trends, customer behavior, and financial performance. By being well-informed and engaged, you'll be able to make the most of this workshop and develop a solid strategy for a successful future.

01. **Business financial statements:** This should include balance sheets, income statements, and cash flow statements, covering at least the past few years.

02. **Market analysis:** Participants should be prepared to present data on the current state of their market and any potential threats to their business.

03. **Customer data:** This should include information on the demographics, behaviors, and needs of the business's core customers.

04. **Staffing information:** Participants should have data on current staffing levels, salaries, and benefits, as well as any plans for future hiring or layoffs.

05. **Supply chain analysis:** Participants should be prepared to discuss their current suppliers, the cost and availability of the goods and services they provide, and any potential risks or challenges to their supply chain.

06. **Sales and marketing strategies:** Participants should be prepared to discuss their current sales and marketing efforts, and what changes they would make in the event of a recession.

07. **P&L analysis:** Participants should have a clear understanding of their revenue, expenses, and profits, and be prepared to discuss ways to improve their P&L during a recession.

08. **Cash flow analysis:** Participants should be prepared to discuss their current cash flow situation, including any debt obligations, and develop a plan for managing their cash flow during a recession.

09. **SWOT analysis:** Participants should be prepared to discuss the strengths, weaknesses, opportunities, and threats of their business, and how these factors could impact their performance during a recession.

10. **Business Strategy:** Participants should have a clear understanding of their current business plan, including their goals, strategies, and tactics, and be prepared to discuss how they would modify their plan in the event of a recession.

Pro Tip: Brainstorm any other areas you think are critical or unique to your business and be ready to talk about them.

Recession Resistant Agenda

This comprehensive workshop agenda has been developed based on years of experience and proven success in helping businesses prepare for and weather economic recessions. It is designed to provide a comprehensive and hands-on approach to safeguarding your business and ensuring its continued success in uncertain times. While every business is unique, the core elements of this agenda have been tried and tested to deliver results. Of course, we encourage you to adapt the agenda to suit the specific needs of your business, but we strongly recommend that you maintain the core elements that make this workshop effective.

Time	Description
30 Min.	**Intro and Overview of the Day** • Introduce the purpose and goals of the workshop • Provide a brief overview of the agenda and what participants can expect to learn • Set expectations for participation and engagement throughout the day • Highlight the importance of preparing facts and data prior to the workshop for the best outcome
2 Hours	**Recession War Game** • Run a simulated recession scenario to help participants understand how a recession might affect their business • Encourage participants to make assumptions and take calculated risks to test their assumptions • Debrief and analyze the results of the simulation • Identify key learning points and areas of improvement
1.5 Hours	**Assumptions and Core Customer** • Based on the results of the recession war game, identify key assumptions that were made during the simulation • Analyze the business's customer base and define the core customer • Discuss what the core customer wants and how to optimize for their needs • Create a plan to ensure that the business is serving its core customer effectively
30 Min.	**Lunch**
1 Hour	**Staff Assessment** • Review the current staffing levels and costs • Discuss values and priorities around staffing decisions. • Develop a plan for cost cutting that can be activated if necessary • Identify immediate actions that can be taken to prepare for a potential recession
1 Hour	**P&L Analysis** • Review the current P&L and identify areas to focus on • Discuss any sacred cows that might need to be addressed in a recession • Develop a plan to improve the P&L and identify immediate actions that can be taken • Consider alternative revenue streams or new product offerings to diversify the business
1 Hour	**Cash Flow** • Explore potential options for managing cash flow during a recession • Develop a plan to improve the cash flow and identify immediate actions that can be taken • Discuss debt management and investment strategies to build a war chest for a potential recession • Consider alternative financing options, such as grants, loans, or investment opportunities, to improve cash flow
30 Min.	**War Room and the Plan** • Identify key performance indicators (KPIs) or metrics to monitor the plan's success • Assign roles and responsibilities for leading the charge • Discuss what execution looks like and how progress will be tracked • Consider regular check-ins and progress reports to ensure that the plan is on track
30 Min.	**Wrap Up and Additional Tasks** • Summarize the key takeaways from the workshop • Identify any additional actions or tasks that need to be completed to fully implement the plan • Provide additional resources or support to help participants continue preparing for a potential recession.

www.growprofitordie.com

Additional Areas *for* Resistance

This page lists a set of additional areas that participants could consider adding to their recession preparedness workshop. However, it's important to keep in mind that time is limited and adding too many sessions could result in insufficient time to delve into each topic in sufficient detail. It's recommended to prioritize and choose only the most relevant topics that align with the specific needs and objectives of the business, while being mindful of the available time.

- *Pricing*
  In this session, participants will delve into their current pricing strategy and how it may need to change during a recession. They will explore pricing techniques to help them stay competitive and profitable during economic downturns.

- *Strategy*
  Participants will examine their existing strategy and make any necessary adjustments to ensure its resilience in a recession.

- *Decision Making and Seat of Power*
  This session will look at decision-making processes and who holds the power to make those decisions in the company. Participants will learn how to make effective decisions during a recession, who should be involved, and what kind of input is required from different teams.

- *Things we WON'T Do, and Things we WILL Do*
  This session will help participants identify the actions they need to avoid during a recession, as well as the actions they must take to protect their business. They will develop a clear plan for what they will and won't do in a recession.

- *Sales Team Management*
  This session will examine the role of the sales team in a recession. Participants will explore how to manage their sales team effectively, how to motivate them and how to measure their performance.

- *Your Personal and Business Calendar*
  This session will help participants understand the importance of having a clear calendar of personal and business activities during a recession. Participants will explore how to prioritize activities, how to schedule necessary meetings, and how to create a routine that will help them stay on track, and NOT "stay" busy.

- *Necessary Meetings and Meeting Rules for Recession*
  In this session, participants will explore the types of meetings that are critical for success during a recession, and the rules for those meetings. They will also reinforce the importance of keeping those meetings focused, productive, and efficient.

- *How we Measure Opportunities and Act on Them*
  This session will help participants learn how to measure opportunities and act on them effectively. They will learn about the importance of monitoring key metrics, how to track progress, and how to use data to make informed decisions.

Additional Areas *for* Resistance

- **People Assessment**
  In this session, participants will review the existing team and have the hard conversations now, as opposed to during the recession. Which team members are performing well? Is the company overstaffed?

- **Supply Chain Management**
  Reviewing your current suppliers and exploring alternative sources for critical products and services.

- **Digital Transformation**
  Examining how technology and digital tools can help your business remain competitive and continue to grow during a recession.

- **Market and Industry Analysis**
  Understanding the broader economic landscape and what shifts may be in store for your industry and market.

- **Leadership and Communication**
  Examining how your leadership style and communication strategies can impact your business during a recession.

- **Additional P&L Work**
  Cost Cutting and Resource Optimization - Identifying areas where costs can be reduced and resources reallocated to maximize efficiency and maintain profitability.

- **Business Networking and Collaboration**
  Building relationships with other businesses and organizations that could be critical partners during a recession. Creating and expanding on your channel is critical.

- **Diversification and New Market Expansion**
  Exploring opportunities for expanding into new markets or diversifying your product or service offerings to mitigate the impact of a recession. Warning!! Making big changes during a recession is risky and tricky, but planning for them reduces risk significantly. Now is the time to try a pivot.

- **Additional Core Customer Work**
  Customer Retention and Loyalty - Developing strategies for retaining customers and keeping them

Summary of Recession Resistant

This workshop is designed to help medium-sized businesses prepare for and navigate a future recession. This agenda focuses on running a Recession War Game, analyzing your core customer, assessing staff, analyzing P&L statements, managing cash flow, and building a comprehensive plan. Additionally, participants are encouraged to tailor the workshop to their specific needs by adding in additional hour-long sessions.

> *A Note on Facilitation: Having a dedicated facilitator, either from within the company or outside, is crucial to the success of the workshop. This person can provide the necessary guidance and support throughout the workshop, ensuring that the participants stay focused and on track. Additionally, a facilitator can help to identify any areas where additional information or data may be needed, and can provide practical advice and support to help the workshop run smoothly. With a skilled facilitator at the helm, participants can feel confident that the workshop will be a valuable and effective tool.*

Facilitator Best Practices

1. Clearly define objectives and desired outcomes for the workshop.
2. Plan a well-structured agenda that allows for interactive activities, group discussions, and individual reflection.
3. Prepare engaging and interactive activities to keep participants engaged.
4. Ensure materials are organized and readily available for each session.
5. Encourage participation and facilitate group discussions to encourage collaboration and diverse perspectives.
6. Be flexible and adjust the agenda as needed based on the needs of the group.
7. Manage time effectively to ensure all objectives are met within the allotted time frame.
8. Foster a supportive and inclusive environment where all participants feel heard and valued.
9. Encourage open and honest communication and manage conflicts effectively.
10. Provide opportunities for participants to reflect on their learning and apply it to their work.
11. Offer clear and concise explanations and facilitate discussions that are relevant to the participants' work.
12. Provide a comfortable and professional environment for the workshop.
13. Continuously evaluate the workshop's effectiveness and make adjustments as needed.
14. End the workshop with a review of key takeaways and action steps for participants to implement after the workshop.

We hope that this workshop has provided valuable insights and tools to help you prepare for a future recession. Red Wagon is here to help facilitate or provide additional content to support your business during these challenging times. We wish you all the best in your endeavors!

— WADE.

RECESSION-RESISTANT INFOGRAPH

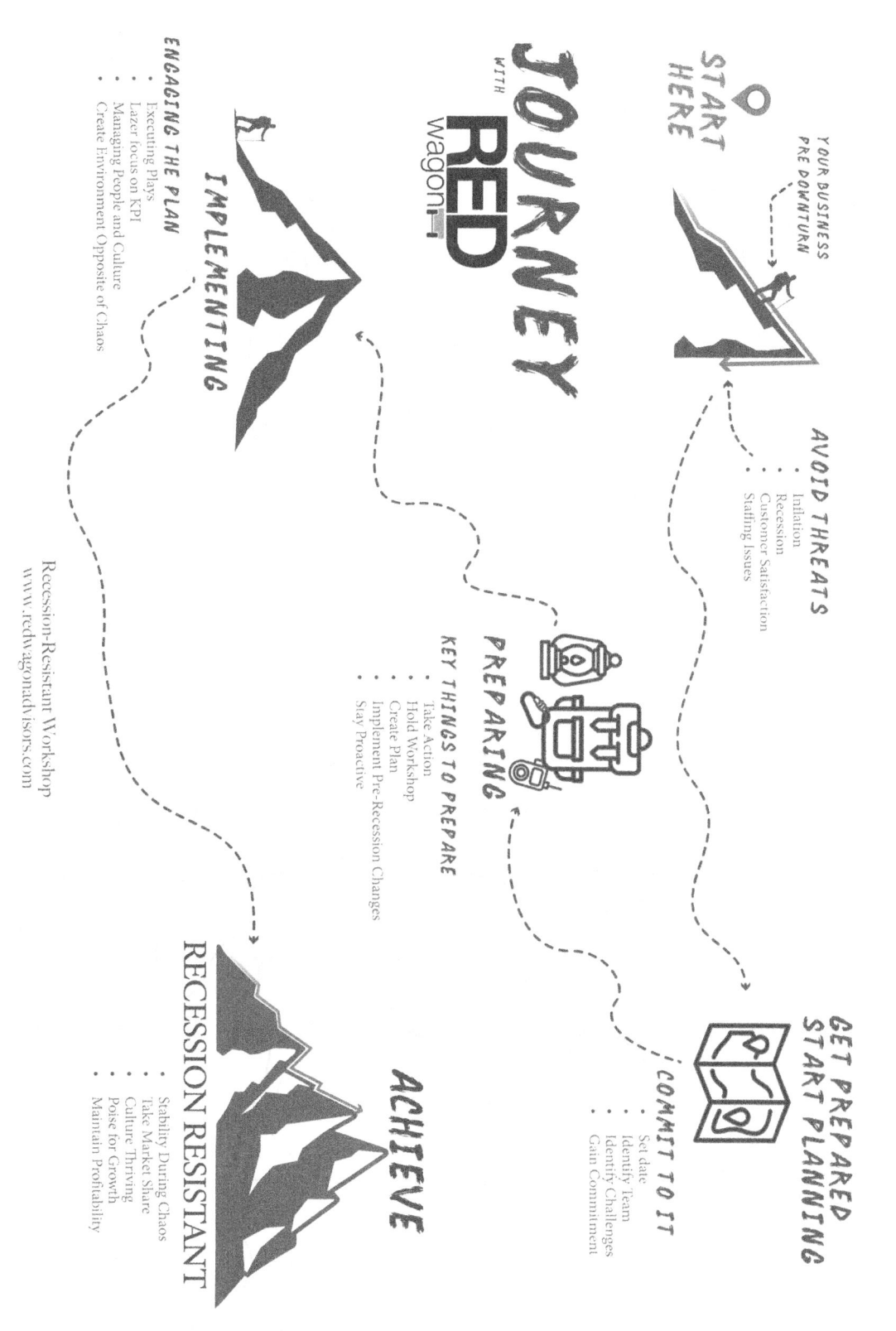

JOURNEY with RED wagon

START HERE — Your Business Pre Downturn

AVOID THREATS
- Inflation
- Recession
- Customer Satisfaction
- Staffing Issues

COMMIT TO IT
- Set date
- Identify Team
- Identify Challenges
- Gain Commitment

GET PREPARED START PLANNING

PREPARING — KEY THINGS TO PREPARE
- Take Action
- Hold Workshop
- Create Plan
- Implement Pre-Recession Changes
- Stay Proactive

IMPLEMENTING — ENGAGING THE PLAN
- Executing Plays
- Lazer focus on KPI
- Managing People and Culture
- Create Environment Opposite of Chaos

ACHIEVE — RECESSION RESISTANT
- Stability During Chaos
- Take Market Share
- Culture Thriving
- Poise for Growth
- Maintain Profitability

Recession-Resistant Workshop
www.redwagonadvisors.com

www.growprofitordie.com

COMING SOON

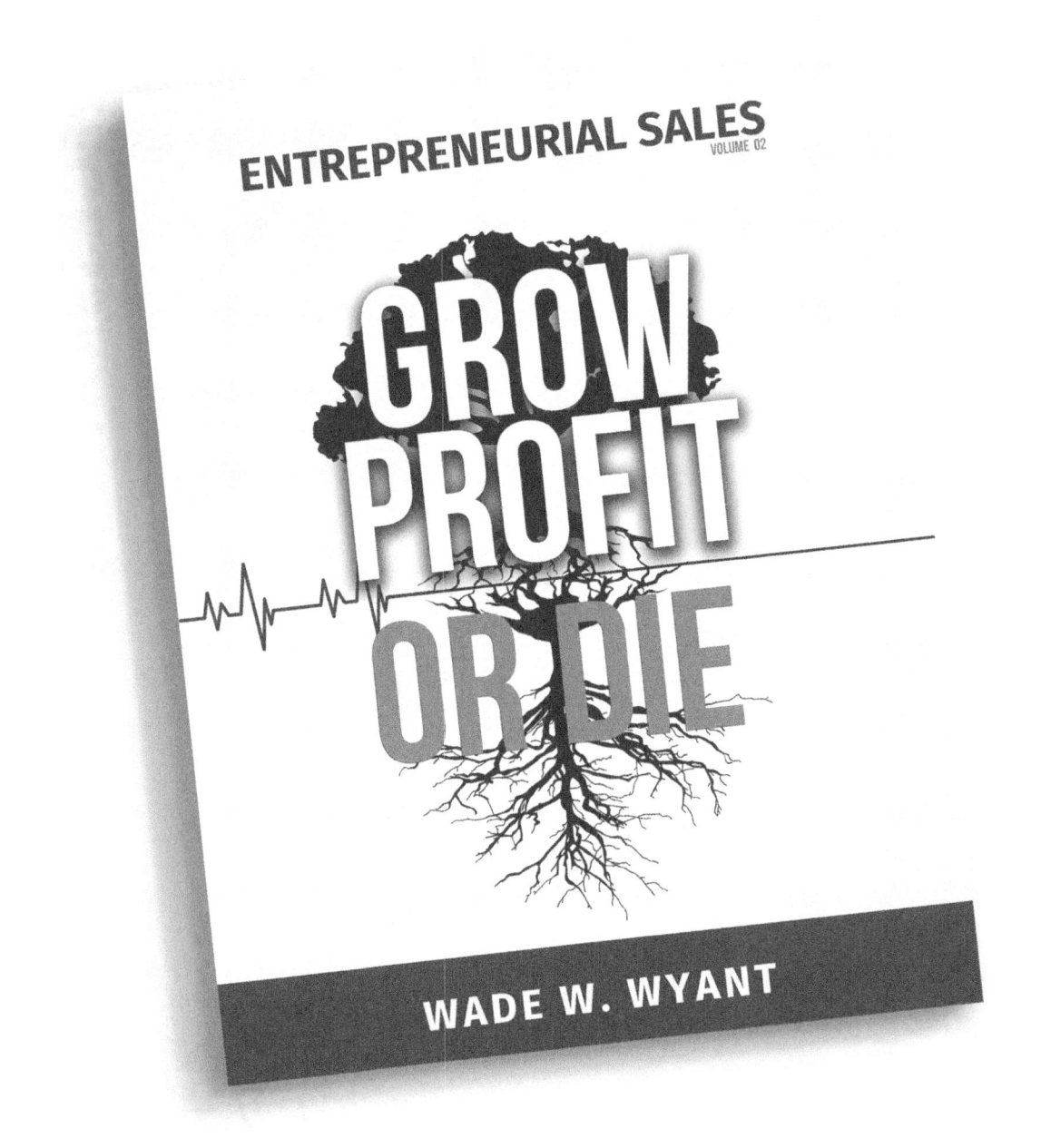

"I'm excited for this next book, I know it will help any entrepeneur."

- Wade Wyant, author of Wake-Up Call and Advisor for Red Wagon Advisors

www.growprofitordie.com

INSIGHTS FOR ENTREPRENEURS TO HAVE MORE FREEDOM, REDUCE DRAMA, AND SCALE THEIR BUSINESS

"This book expands the reach of his business coaching, and it's a must-read book for every entrepreneur. *Wake-Up Call* is an excellent addition to the Scaling Up family of books."

- Verne Harnish, Founder Entrepreneurs' Organization (EO) and author of *Scaling Up (Rockefeller Habits 2.0)*

www.growprofitordie.com

FOCUS ON BECOMING RESISTANT

Congratulations on taking proactive steps to prepare your business for potential economic challenges. Our workbook guides you through ways to facilitate a workshop that will bolster your profit growth and equip you for any future recession.

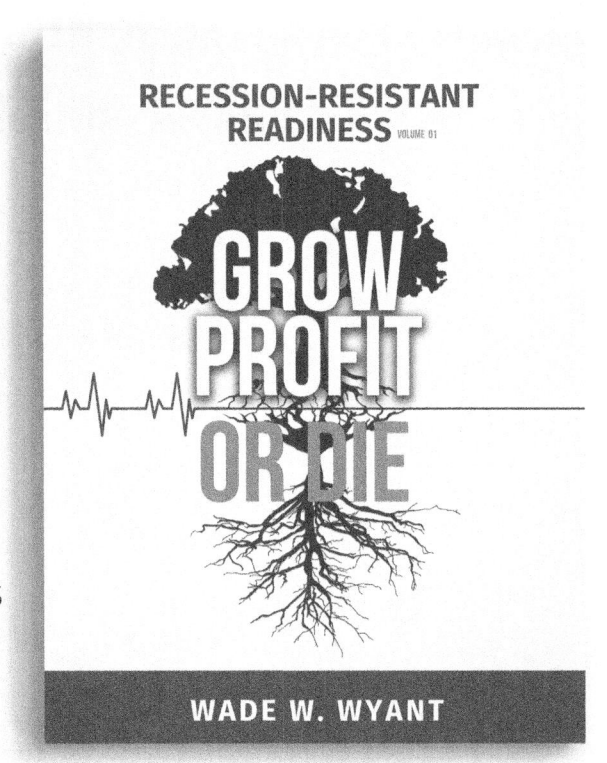

- Clearly define objectives and desired outcomes for the workshop.

- Build a well-structured agenda that allows for interactive activities, group discussions, and individual reflection.

- Focus on key areas such as running a Recession War Game, analyzing your core customer, assessing staffing, analyzing P&L statements, managing cash flow, and building a comprehensive plan.

- Identify areas for growth and develop a solid plan for success.

- Don't miss this opportunity to secure your business's future!

Contact Red Wagon Advisors Today
www.growprofitordie.com

BECOME RECESSION RESISTANT TODAY

CALL FOR PRICING
INTENSE WORKSHOP FOR UP TO 10 PEOPLE

LEARN HOW TO BECOME RECESSION RESISTANT

OVERVIEW

STRATEGY

PEOPLE

CASH

ABOUT WADE WYANT

Wade Wyant has 20 plus years experience as a CEO and entrepreneur. He has managed through two other major recessions, and is ready to share what he learned to help your team.

Our workshop is designed to take the principles we have learned working with Scaling Up and writing our book *Wake-Up Call* to bring you practical work you can do today to be recession restant!

THE BENEFITS

Specific to your Business
Our workshop includes, an assessment of your current maturity, assessment of your cashflow position, pre-work to help you discover what is needed to be resistant and resilient in the coming recession.

One Day Workshop
We deliver a full-day workshop with your team, that will generate a plan specific to you and your needs. Post the event, you will have a coaching call with Wade, and he will deliver your final plan and ensure you are ready.

Recession Resistant Workshop
- Pre-workshop assessments
- Pre-workshop homework
- One day workshop with your leadership team
- Post workshop plan
- Post workshop coaching with Wade

Additional Tools to Help Your Business
Articles Published In *Wake-Up Call*

www.growprofitordie.com

GROW OR DIE: THE MOST ABUSED PHRASE IN BUSINESS

I have mixed emotions about the phrase "grow or die" in business. On the one hand, it's great advice, and I agree with it 100 percent. However, the problem I have with it is not so much the literal words. It's the way people usually apply it, which typically doesn't lead to the kind of growth companies need to thrive — or to avoid dying.

In fact, "grow or die" is one of the most abused terms in business. A lot of that has to do with the nature of entrepreneurs, who are often more inclined to go-go-go than they are to think about where they're going.

So, when you tell a go-go-go entrepreneur to "grow or die," it begs the question: What does it mean to grow? Too often that entrepreneur will simply assume growth refers to one thing and one thing only — and that's top-line revenue.

Now I'm all about bringing in more revenue. However, it's a mistake to think that's the only form of growth your company needs. It's also a big mistake to think you can become more successful by focusing only on revenue growth and not on the things that typically lead to it.

Growth done right means becoming better in a lot of ways. It means improving in employee engagement. It means enhancing the value you offer your customers. It means conceiving and perfecting products that truly serve a need in the market. It means building a company culture that emphasizes excellence in every aspect of operations.

Chiefly, it means growing profitability first. Absent of this focus on profitability, products, and culture, revenue can become little more than vanity for the owner. Your top line may look good, but if you haven't grown in these other areas, you're not in the strongest position to parlay that higher revenue into real, sustained success.

I can tell you firsthand I won a lot of trophies and got a lot of recognition for revenue growth, but I would give them all back to have had more profitability. There will always be people willing to help you grow your revenue by buying your underpriced product or service. Find a way to grow your business with the right buyers, at the right price, and at the right profitability.

The entrepreneur who's chasing only after higher revenues will tend to put outsized emphasis on sales. He is sure the product or service is great, and that he has exactly the right people, and that all the company needs is more people buying.

This is the entrepreneur who doesn't think there's any definition of growth apart from simply taking in more money. Everything else? He's sure he's got that mastered. In fact, the great companies have often had seasons of growth in which they elevated themselves in different areas. This was true of Apple, where they spent time focusing on employee engagement, then more time focusing on client value. All along the way they kept zeroing in on what they needed to accomplish to become a truly great company.

Many entrepreneurs are relatively young. They're full of energy and they have great ideas, but they're lacking in experience and education, so they may not understand everything that's required to achieve what you can call a growing company. Although there are many areas of growth you should focus on, here are three that make a huge difference:
1. Better products.
2. Better people to deliver the products.
3. Better sales and marketing.

Beyond that, you can add better financial management, better deployment of resources, and better improvement processes. These are all things that lead to more revenue, so they're all part of growth.

If I had to name one thing that would define your priority in growth, it wouldn't be revenue. It would be the value you represent to your customers. Grow in that area, and just about everything else will take care of itself. Of course, to achieve that, you have to grow in all the areas mentioned above — and that will likely require various stages of growth to get you to the goal.

Skipping all this and just focusing on sales gets it exactly backward. When you're truly excellent in all the areas I've described here, the company's offering practically sells itself. I'm not saying you don't need to get out there and market it, but it's not hard to make the sale when the value is that clear. People will always buy what gives them more value and helps them to achieve their goals.

If this is what you mean by growth, then I agree with grow or die. Failing to grow in all these ways will leave you in your competitors' dust, because they will surpass you. Grow or die is a great term as long as you understand there are stages to business growth, and as long as you're committed to what those stages will require of you.

When grow or die just means "bring in more revenue," someone needs to sit down and have a serious talk with the entrepreneur who's pushing that thinking. That's not growth at all. It's an ill-fated attempt to get more people to throw money at you when you haven't done the things that would allow you to say you've earned it.

By the way, the ultimate prize for all this isn't more revenue. It's more profit. If you want a monetary measure of your business's success, that's it. Lots of companies bring in revenue but don't make much profit, because they haven't grown in the areas we've discussed here. Do the hard work, and accomplish the real growth, and then your profit will prove to be a much more satisfying one.

Wake-Up Call: *Grow profit or die.*

Most Partnerships Die, And Most Partners Don't See It Coming

It's easy to feel good about the idea of a business partnership. Two friends, two acquaintances, or two professional associates who share a vision . . . starting a business and conquering the world together.

Then one day, way in the future, they'll be able to tell the story of their partnership and how they couldn't have done all they did if they hadn't done it together.

It's too bad almost none of them end up that way, but it's not that surprising either. Most partnerships aren't built to last, because businesses change, and people change. Sometimes one of the most unproductive things you can do is try to preserve a 50-50 partnership in a business that's evolving away from it.

I'm not opposed to partnerships per se. I have simply observed over time that almost all of them end up dead at some point. If you're thinking about becoming part of a partnership, maybe what I have to say here will help you prepare for some eventualities that have happened to many others in your position.

If you decide not to become part of a partnership because of this chapter, that's fine, too. My point here is not to persuade you one way or the other. It's just to make sure you're aware of what has happened to many who have gone before you.

One of the most fundamental weaknesses of partnerships is that they tend to be set up by attorneys. Now I have nothing against legal professionals. They play their role very well. However, when an attorney sets up a partnership, he or she deals with the logical aspect of the contract. An attorney invariably misses the psychological aspects, and those are usually the seeds of the partnership's demise. Legal constructs don't run partnerships. Entrepreneurs do. And while entrepreneurs can be great visionaries and hard workers — and without a doubt, high achievers — they can also be naïve about some things.

www.growprofitordie.com

One of those things is the reality that the partnership is probably going to end at some point. I realize no one wants to come right out and say that when they're just getting started. You want to express all the confidence in the world that you're in it for the long haul. Maybe you feel like it would be a betrayal to include exit protocols in your partnership agreement, but it's a huge mistake not to because things change.

For example, it's common in the early days of a partnership for the partners to take modest salaries to keep costs low. I once consulted with a company whose partners did that at first, but soon one of the partners became a parent. He felt he needed to draw a higher salary to support his wife and baby. The other partner was single, and he saw no need to take a raise. However, they had to make the same money because they were 50-50. The two partners disagreed over salaries, and it became a point of conflict.

Neither was right or wrong. They were just in different positions, and they had different priorities. The partner whose wife had a baby wasn't wrong to become a father. The other partner wasn't wrong to remain single. It was just who they were, but it made the partnership structure harder to sustain. (They didn't make it past three years, by the way.)

Partners who don't talk through the complexities of the partnership — including different scenarios that could affect the business and their roles together — are setting themselves up for a difficult dissolution down the road.

However, even if you do have that discussion, there are some things a legal agreement can't prepare you for: Humans get offended. They have egos. They want things, and they change over time. What made all the sense in the world to you at 30 makes no sense at all when you're 45. What you once were sure of, doesn't seem so certain at a different point in time.

Once you were willing to work 24/7 to build the business. Now you want a vacation. However, your partner might not care about taking a vacation, and you're concerned you'll seem like the lesser contributor if you go on one.

Once you were ready to work until you had both feet in the grave. Now you're starting to think retirement doesn't sound so bad, but you didn't structure the partnership to account for that. So, what do you do?

To make matters worse, it's not only people who change. Businesses change, too. Often, the basic structure and value proposition you started with give way to different directions as you learn things — positive and negative — from your experiences.

Let's say you were originally going to sell auto parts to local retailers, and one of the partners had great connections with all the retailers, so that partner got the job of selling. However, you soon realized the industry doesn't work the way you thought, and there were better strategies for distributing your product. So, you had to make an adjustment. Nothing wrong with that. It happens all the time. However, the sales partner didn't have connections with people in the new distribution channels, so suddenly his role isn't what either of you expected. The new role probably doesn't justify 50 percent of the profits.

However, he's 50 percent owner, so what do you do now? The two partners are no longer as complementary as they once were, and it's not so easy to retrofit them into the new realities.

Finally, there is this uncomfortable reality: Partnerships that start with friendship can't necessarily be sustained over the long-term with that same friendship, because friendships evolve based on experiences. Your best friends in college might not still be your closest friends once you're married and raising kids. As you get older, you move to different stages of life, and you share different kinds of experiences with other people. If you become business partners with a friend, your friendship isn't going to be the same in two years, because you've both been through different things. It might be better. It might be worse, but it won't be the same.

Keeping a strong relationship with your partner is something you both need to work on frequently. The partnership will only work if both are willing to put in the necessary effort. Basically, a business run by partners requires the constant maintenance of two things — the business and an interpersonal relationship.

A business run by just one owner requires just the maintenance of the business. That doesn't mean partnerships can never work. Obviously, some do go the distance. However, yours is far less likely to do so if you don't understand these issues up front. And if your partnership does come to an end at some point, that just means it's like most of the others.

When forming a partnership, think about all the complexities before writing a contract with an attorney. How will you handle changes in the business? What will you do if one partner wants to retire? What type of exit protocols do you need? Enlist your attorney's help with the details in the contract only after you have agreed and thought through each stage.

Wake-Up Call: *All partnerships eventually end, but most don't end well. (If you think your partnership is just okay, you're probably in more trouble than you think.)*

The Strategic Planning Letdown, And How To Avoid It

Have you ever felt a letdown after Christmas? You know you shouldn't feel that way because you have all these nice new things, right? Then you realize that what's most special about Christmas is the experience — the anticipation, the sharing, the revealing, and the time with family. At some point, with all that behind you, you kick back and look at all your new stuff. You feel a little deflated because Christmas itself was the best part and now it's over. I think this is a pretty close approximation of what many companies experience, and it's called Strategic Planning Letdown.

If you do strategic planning on a regular basis (and you certainly should), then you know it can be a fun, exciting and even inspiring experience. You go off-site, maybe for a day or two. You do some fun team-building exercises, and you set big goals that you expect to pay off in the form of a realized vision for the company's future. By the time this strategic planning session is over, you might feel a little exhausted, but it's a great form of exhaustion because you can't wait to get to actually implement those goals and strategies.

Then you get back to the office. You've got 1,000 emails in your inbox. A supplier didn't come through with a shipment you needed. A customer is unhappy about something, and it has to be dealt with right away.

Sure, you want to do all the things you talked about in strategic planning, but today you need to take care of all this. Maybe tomorrow. Actually, tomorrow looks crazy, too. Maybe the next day. Or maybe not . . . Before long, just about everyone who took part in the strategic planning session feels like the session itself was the high point.

There's little to no follow-up. Why? It's because no one feels they have the time, or because there's no plan to put the ideas into action. Or, maybe it's because no one is taking charge to make sure it happens. It could even be some combination of these things, but as the disappointment of the strategic planning outcome sets in, people can become disillusioned.

www.growprofitordie.com

Coming up with a big and inspiring new plan is great, but if the company doesn't show it can follow through, then the result could be worse than if you'd never done it in the first place. Now people will question whether it's worth their time to participate in future planning sessions since the track record suggests the company will put the giant pads of paper containing all the ideas in a closet somewhere — and never act on them. This is all very unnecessary. When I take companies through strategic planning sessions, one crucial step is to make sure there are clear action steps to follow thesession. We identify who is in charge of moving them forward. We assign action steps with timelines.

We even make sure these assignments are incorporated into the company's regular planning system, which will work whether the system is sophisticated like Trello or as basic as a typed-up to-do list. I have a friend who owns a company consisting of two full-time employees. They share their to-do lists on a Google Drive document.

For a company like this, following up on strategic planning priorities would get a big push forward by simply putting those items on the Google doc and making sure they don't get taken off. With my clients, we always have a follow-up session 90 days after the initial one. So, there's a built-in incentive to move the priorities forward. No one wants to show up at the follow-up session and say they didn't do any of the things they agreed to do at the first one.

Certainly, the CEO doesn't want to show up at the follow-up session and have everyone say the CEO dropped the ball because that's an indictment of the CEO's leadership.

The key to all this is to make sure the strategic planning session is more than just an uplifting, emotional, and visionary experience. It's fine for it to be all of that, but it also needs to be the start of an ongoing action initiative with real measurements of success.

Coming out of the planning session, if you can see how you'll undertake the action steps and achieve the goals, you've done a good job. If you've thought through the hurdles and you know how you'll tackle them, you're in a great position to get the most out of these efforts. If you return to the office with a different perspective on what you need to do and how you'll spend your days, then all this has been an excellent investment of time and money.

However, think all this through before you wrap up the session. Otherwise, the letdown is a real possibility, and you'll wonder why you ever did it in the first place.

Wake-Up Call: *Don't get caught up in the emotional excitement of strategy. Leave room to execute your vision.*

SHARKS ARE IN THE WATER: WILL YOU BE ONE OF THEM OR THEIR PREY?

There are sharks in the water. If you're in business in the 2020s, there's no escaping that. The only question is whether you're one of them – or if you're their prey. In a decade like the 2020s, a lot of businesses are in precarious positions. They might have made questionable decisions for years, but good economic conditions allowed them to escape major consequences for a time. In a decade like this, your weaknesses get exposed, and you sometimes find yourself in a position where you can't refuse any offer that gives you an escape hatch.

That's where the sharks come in. There are always people looking for good bargains on businesses. They want your property. They want your fixtures. They want access to your clients. They probably have the ability to shore up the operation in ways that you can't, and they know you're not in a position to turn down their offer.

So, they're looking to buy, at a price that's very favorable to them. They're sharks, and I mean that without the slightest hint of condemnation. There's a reason sharks rule the ocean. They're a crucial part of the ecosystem, and it wouldn't work without them. Sharks in business are doing what smart people always do. They're responding rationally to incentives. If a business is in precarious shape because it doesn't have a good balance sheet, or it hasn't been keeping its numbers as it should have, or it can't seem to make its cash flow work, the shark takes notice of these critical points.

The shark also knows that the assets of that business are probably worth more than its current leadership. Better leadership could turn it around. Sharks only want to make a minimal investment in a business like this because a) its performance doesn't justify any more than that, and b) the owner wouldn't be smart to hold out for any more than that.

So, I'm talking to the people who own businesses that might be targets of the sharks. How do you recognize these sharks? Often, they have made their money by coming into generational wealth or have gotten their money somehow on the sidelines. They don't want to build a business. They want to take over one that someone else has built but is having trouble leading to prosperity.

These sharks could invest in a business for a multiple on EBITA, which is the kind of business acquisition you'd hope to be part of if you're the seller. However, the sharks don't want to do that. They want to take on distressed businesses that they can get for mere book value, or maybe just the straight value of the assets and the cash on hand. In some cases, they'll want to take over your business, but they won't offer any more than to cover your payroll for the coming year.

That's quite a bargain, wouldn't you say? Acquiring all a company's assets just for keeping people employed? These sharks have long memories. They know that in 2001, when we experienced the last recession similar to the current one (in other words, not precipitated by a financial market meltdown like in 2008), a lot of businesses changed hands for very little money.

Do you want to avoid being prey for sharks like this? Then do the following:

First, look at your cash conversion cycle, or CCC. That seems so fundamental. No one should even need to be told to do it, right? But you have to tell NBA players to practice their free throws because they don't like to. I know better than to assume that everyone in business does this. Very few look at the full maturity of their CCCs. (For more details about CCC, read the "Cash" section in Scaling Up.[1]) Business owners usually just look at how quickly they can get one portion of that cycle back by collecting on current receivables.

However, you need to look at the full cash conversion cycle from top to bottom. Here are some questions to ask as you look at your cash conversion cycle: How do you get sales? How do you make things or deliver services more quickly? How can you collect the money faster? At the other end, how do you stretch your payables as long as possible without being unethical about it? If you don't have this mastered, you are ripe for a shark to come and get you.

Another solution is the "Power of One," which is discussed in Scaling Up.[2] You want to look at the seven key financial levers that you can influence to achieve more corporate success, such as increasing price, volume, and the number of days to pay creditors.[3] You also want to consider decreasing overhead, stock days, cost of goods sold, and length of time to collect money from clients.[4] If you're not inspecting every one of these in your weekly management meetings, you're in trouble.

Finally, you need to be in frequent and good communication with your bank. There has rarely been a time when the business community has had more access to capital than it does right now. If you're not talking to your banker, you could be missing out on an opportunity to either save or expand your business.

Now let's say you're on top of all this. Your finances are sound, and your performance is solid. In this case, you have no need to think about these sharks, correct?

Wrong. If this is the case, you should be one of the sharks. The natural direction of business is always growth, and if you're not taking advantage of high-value opportunities to expand a well-run operation, you're missing the chance to strengthen the business community as a whole, while rewarding yourself in the process.

The business owners who can't get these things right are ultimately doing no favors for their employees, their customers, or even themselves.

If you are one of these business owners who are not getting it right, you're probably better off taking a shark's offer than continuing to struggle. And the shark can probably shore up your business in a way that you can't – because if you could, you would have already done so.

Sharks are not shy about hunting for their prey. So, if you are struggling, you'd better start doing it right. You know how sharks get when they smell blood.

Wake-Up Call: *Vince Lombardi started training camp with these words, "Gentlemen, this is a football." Today I want to start your wake-up call with, "Readers, this is a balance sheet."*

Citations

Introduction

1. Harnish, Verne. *Scaling Up: How a Few Companies Make It … and Why the Rest Don't.* Gazelles Inc., 2015.

2. Wickman, Gino. *Traction: Get a Grip on Your Business.* BenBella Books, 2011.

Chapter 1

1. Locke, Taylor. "Jeff Bezos: This Is the 'smartest Thing We Ever Did' at Amazon." CNBC, CNBC, 15 Oct. 2019, www.cnbc.com/2019/10/14/jeff-bezos-this-is-the-smartest-thing-we-ever-did-at-amazon.html.

Chapter 2

1. Daly, Jack. *Hyper Sales Growth: Street-Proven Systems & Processes: How to Grow Quickly & Profitably.* ForbesBooks, 2017.

Chapter 4

1. Bloom, Robert H., and Dave Conti. *The inside Advantage: The Strategy That Unlocks the Hidden Growth in Your Business.* McGraw-Hill, 2008.

2. Bloom, *The Inside Advantage.*

3. Harnish, *Scaling Up.*

4. Lencioni, Patrick. *The Five Dysfunctions of a Team: A Workshop for Team Leaders*, Pfeiffer, San Francisco, CA, 2012, pp. 202–203.

5. "Fire Bullets, Then Cannonballs." *Jim Collins - Concepts - Fire Bullets, Then Cannon balls*, www.jimcollins.com/concepts/fire-bullets-then-cannonballs.html#:~:text=First%2C%20you%20fire%20bullets%20(low,the%20calibrated%20line%20of%20sight. Accessed 12 Oct. 2023.

6. "The Power of Virtual Integration: An Interview with Dell Computer's Michael Dell." *Harvard Business Review*, 1 Aug. 2014, hbr.org/1998/03/the-power-of-virtual-integration-an-interview-with-dell-computers-michael-dell#:~:text=Michael%20Dell%20began%20in%201984,and%20build%20products%20to%20orde

7. Harnish, *Scaling Up*.

Article: Sharks Are in the Water: Will You Be One of Them or Their Prey?

1. Harnish, Verne. *Scaling up: How a Few Companies Make It … and Why the Rest Don't*. (Gazelles Inc., 2015).

2. Harnish, Scaling Up, 219-233.

3. Harnish, Scaling Up, 231.

4. Harnish, Scaling Up, 231.

Get In Touch

RED wagon

CONTACT US

Email : wadewyant@redwagonadvisors.com

Website : www.redwagonadvisors.com

Website : www.growprofitordie.com

FOLLOW US

Instagram : Instagram.com/redwagoninc

Facebook : Facebook.com/redwagonadvisors

LinkedIn : Linkedin.com/in/wadewyant

Connect with Wade on Minnect

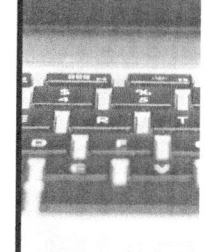